Stage 2

Literacy Lesson

Teacher's Guide

Diana Bentley and Dee Reid

Heinemann

Heinemann Educational Publishers
Halley Court, Jordan Hill, Oxford OX2 8EJ
a division of Reed Educational & Professional Publishing Limited

OXFORD MELBOURNE AUCKLAND
JOHANNESBURG BLANTYRE GABORONE
IBADAN PORTSMOUTH (NH) USA CHICAGO

Series Editors: Diana Bentley and Dee Reid

Cover illustration by Martin Chatterton 1998

First published 1998

02 01 00 99 98
10 9 8 7 6 5 4 3 2 1

British Library Cataloguing in Publication Data
A catalogue record for this book is available from the British Library.

Literacy Lesson Fiction Teacher's Guide Stage 2
ISBN 0 435 09337 1

(Essential Texts Anthology Stage 2
ISBN 0 435 11484 0)
(Essential Texts Anthology Stage 2, six pack
ISBN 0 435 09313 4)

Printed and bound in the UK

Contents

Lesson plans for the *Essential Texts Anthology* pieces

Welcome to Literacy World

Literacy World is a complete literacy programme for 7–11 year olds which includes both fiction and poetry and non-fiction texts. It is structured around the format of the Literacy Hour, and linked closely to the teaching objectives contained in the *Framework for Teaching* document as part of the National Literacy Strategy. Because it is fundamentally a balanced literacy programme, schools not implementing the *Framework* document can also use it.

This brief introduction will set out the aims of Literacy World, and, most importantly, how we envisage its use in the junior classroom.

Chart of Components

FICTION *for each of Years 3–6*

WHOLE CLASS TEACHING

Literacy Lesson Teacher's Guide ▶ **Essential Texts Anthology** ▶ **3 Literacy Skills Big Books**

GROUP WORK

2 Novels | 2 Short Story Collections | 1 Play Anthology — **Guided Reading Books** ▶ **Pupil Skills Book** ▶ **Guided Reading Teacher's Cards**

NON-FICTION *for each of Years 3–6*

WHOLE CLASS TEACHING

Literacy Lesson Teacher's Guide ▶ **2 Literacy Skills Big Books** ▶ Encyclopedias | Dictionaries — **Reference Texts** *(available as both Big and Little Books)*

GROUP WORK

Information Book | Information Book | Information Book | Information Book — **4 Guided Reading Information Books** ▶ **Guided Reading Teacher's Cards**

How to use the Literacy World fiction components together

❶ Choose your text range from the *Framework* Document.

38 YEAR 4 TERM 1

Range

Fiction and poetry: *Historical stories and short novels; playscripts; poems based on common themes, e.g. space, school, animals, families, feelings, viewpoints.*

Non-Fiction: *A range of text-types from reports and articles in newspapers and magazines, etc.; instructions.*

❷ Choose a matching text from the *Essential Texts Anthology.*

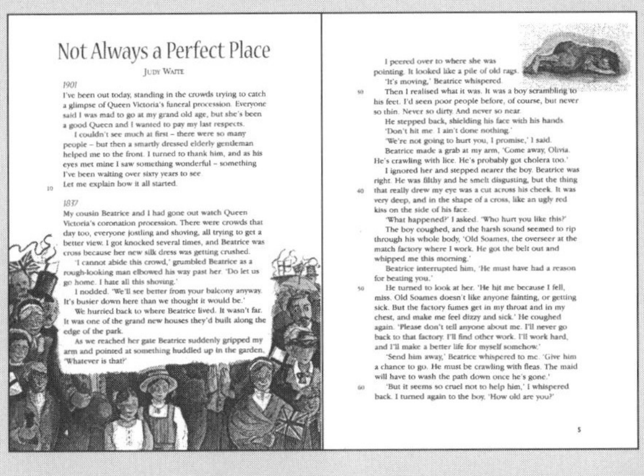

❸ Weekly lesson plans for teaching the text, sentence and word level objectives that develop out of the *Anthology* piece can be found in the *Literacy Lesson Teacher's Guide.*

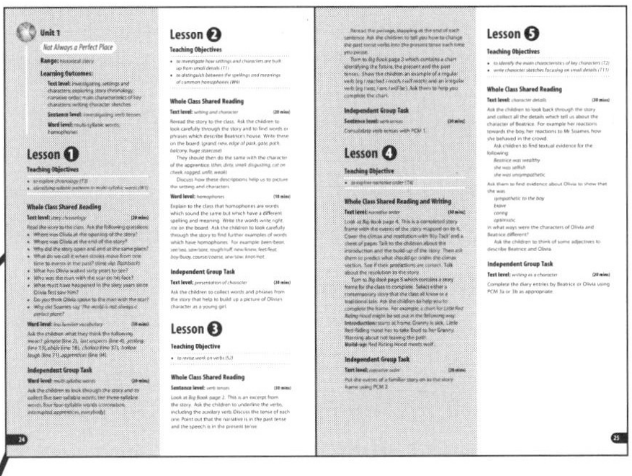

❹ The *Guide* will also show you when to use the accompanying *Literacy Skills Big Book* pages that focus on specific skills.

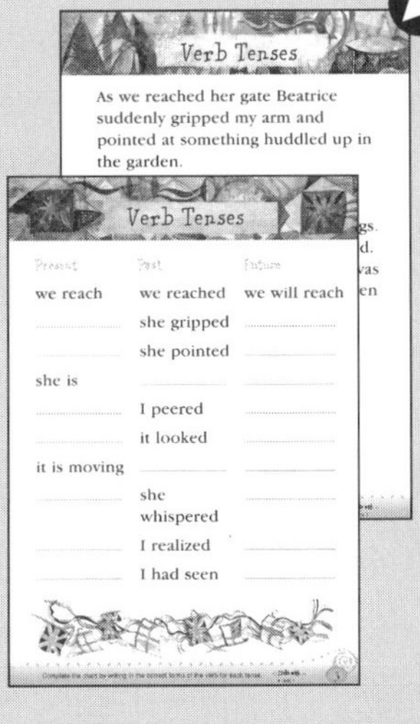

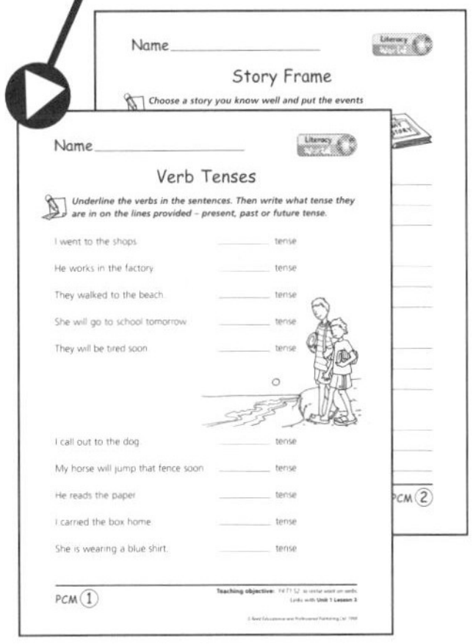

❺ Choose from a range of photocopy masters for follow-up group work linked to the whole class session.

Guided reading and group work

❶ Five graded texts: 2 novels, 2 sets of short stories, 1 play anthology are provided for guided reading sessions.

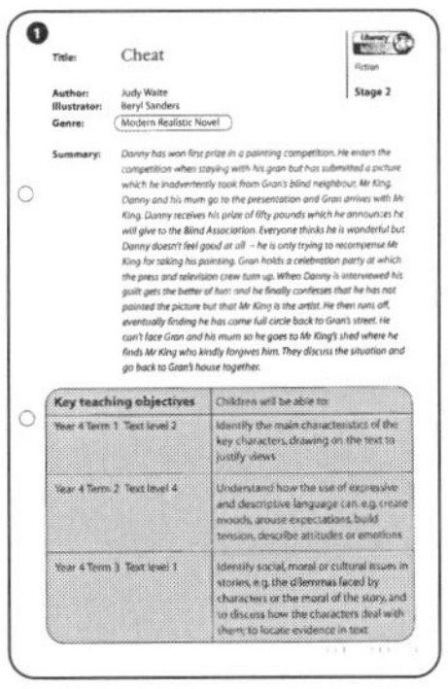

❷ Guided reading cards give you planned lessons linked to teaching objectives using the fiction.

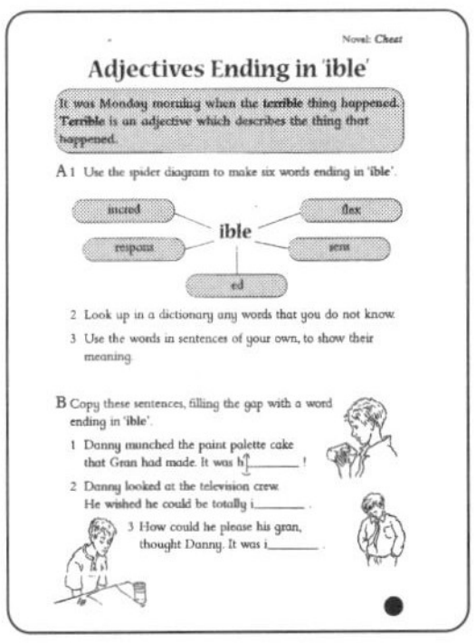

❸ For further options in group work, select from a range of 9 activities linked to each guided reading book.

Shared Reading and Writing

Fiction and poetry – the *Essential Texts Anthology*

At the heart of the fiction side of Literacy World is the *Essential Texts Anthology* of fiction and poetry. It has been organized to follow the termly range requirements set out in the *Framework* and will provide a whole year's worth of shared reading material for fiction and poetry. The texts have been carefully chosen for their appeal to children, their quality and their suitability to deliver a full range of teaching objectives. It has been particularly important for us to choose texts that children will respond to enthusiastically. It is vital to the teaching of literacy that children enjoy reading as well as become more critical, thoughtful readers. The *Anthology* compiler, Brian Moses, is well known as a performance poet and author in his own right and is a familiar visitor to schools.

Access to the text

In order for children to critically evaluate texts, you need to have extracts of quality and some length. This also applies in choosing pieces that will allow you to teach the full range of objectives in the *Framework* document. It is very difficult for children to scan large amounts of text in Big Book form when analysing it in the kind of detail the *Framework* requires for word and sentence level work particularly. The *Essential Texts Anthologies* have therefore been produced as individual pupil books, which we believe is a much more comfortable medium for children to use.

The level of the texts in the *Anthology* is assumed to be higher than the instructional level of an average ability Year 4 pupil. As the teacher models the reading to the children, they are able to cope with texts beyond their reading abilities.

A context for teaching

The *Anthology* piece becomes the context for the whole week's work, and out of it the text, sentence and word level work develops. This work is reinforced in the photocopy masters provided for independent group work. Thus the teaching of specific grammar and vocabulary level work does not become a disembodied activity, but arises naturally as part of the analysis of the text that forms the basis of the week's work.

Using *Essential Texts* and the *Big Books* together

The *Essential Texts Anthology* works in conjunction with the *Literacy Skills Big Books A, B* and *C* (there is one *Big Book* per term). The *Big Books:*

- develop some extracts
- provide contrasting texts or poems for others
- offer specific teaching points at text, sentence and word level
- provide models for shared writing.

Almost always, the context for the *Big Book* work is the *Anthology* piece itself. So if, for example, you wish to concentrate on the teaching of verb tenses, *Big Book* pages 20–22 uses verbs from the *Anthology* piece as its basis for teaching.

Occasionally, a text will not lend itself to the study of a specific piece of grammar or word work and a special *Big Book* page will have been created to do this.

Using the acetate sheets

Sometimes in the *Big Book* we have extracted a smaller piece from the original *Essential Texts* extract to enable you to really focus on a particular skill area. Using the acetate sheet you, or the children, can find and mark specific examples of grammar or vocabulary work from the original extract. We **never** ask the children to focus on both the *Anthology* and the *Big Book* at the same time.

Using the Literacy Lesson Teacher's Guide

For each term, we have provided six weeks of lesson plans for fiction and poetry. Using the particular *Essential Texts* piece (or pieces) as a starting point, the lesson plans offer a coherent delivery of text, sentence and word level work arising out of it. See pages 10–11 for a more detailed breakdown of the lesson plans. Unlike other approaches, we do not offer simply a list of possible activities, but actively mesh them together in a progressive and logical way. We have also built in progression within the teaching across the term, and then across the year, so we recommend that the lessons are taught in the order presented. However, you can also teach them as independent units of work.

We have included approximate timings in order to let you know our assumptions. The timings are not intended to be prescriptive and we would expect teachers to adapt the lessons according to the needs of their own circumstances.

Literacy World does not attempt to deliver every single objective in the *Framework* document, even though it will cover the majority of them. It assumes that teachers will incorporate other methods to deliver some of the objectives, for example in the teaching of spelling. We have also assumed that the revision and consolidation objectives will be developed and monitored by the teacher.

The plenary session

Although Literacy World tries to be very supportive to teachers, we have also assumed a degree of flexibility. We cannot know what is being taught in every literacy hour, and we feel it is important for teachers themselves to decide what they would most like to focus on at the end of the session.

Independent group activities

We feel it is very important that the independent group activities should be linked to the shared work in the first part of the hour. Over the course of the week we suggest five different group tasks. Photocopy masters support three of these activities. One of the photocopiable activities is differentiated. The photocopy masters can be used at the teacher's discretion; on some occasions several groups could be undertaking one activity.

Other group activities are provided in the *Reading and Language Skills Book*. This provides focused text, sentence and word level work linked to the core reader books for the Stage. Succinct explanations of grammar points are provided to really help the children to work independently. Most children should be able to attempt the level A questions in the books, but the B and C questions are to be seen as extension activities for more able children.

Planning and the Literacy Hour

On page 12 of this guide, you will find an example of how one unit from Stage 2 fits into the NLS weekly lesson planner. In the Guided group work, we have included examples from the Stage 2 fiction for use in the Guided Reading sessions. The structure for these sessions can be found in the cards that accompany each book.

How to use the weekly lesson plans

Each unit delivers one week of literacy hour teaching based around the piece from the *Essential Texts Anthology*.

The objectives for each lesson relate directly to the termly *Framework* fiction objectives.

Approximate timings are given to help you plan in even more detail.

A balance of text, sentence and word level objectives is delivered over the week.

Unit 1

Not Always a Perfect Place

Range: historical story

Learning Outcomes:

Text level: investigating settings and characters; exploring story chronology; narrative order; main characteristics of key characters; writing character sketches

Sentence level: investigating verb tenses

Word level: multi-syllabic words; homophones

Lesson 1

Teaching Objectives

- *to explore chronology (T3)*
- *identifying syllabic patterns in multi-syllabic words (W1)*

Whole Class Shared Reading

Text level: *story chronology* **(20 mins)**

Read the story to the class. Ask the following questions:

- Where was Olivia at the opening of the story?
- Where was Olivia at the end of the story?
- Why did the story open and end at the same place?
- What do we call it when stories move from one time to events in the past? (*time slip, flashback*)
- What has Olivia waited sixty years to see?
- Who was the man with the scar on his face?
- What must have happened in the sixty years since Olivia first saw him?
- Do you think Olivia spoke to the man with the scar?
- Why did Soames say *'The world is not always a perfect place?'*

Word level: *less familiar vocabulary* **(10 mins)**

Ask the children what they think the following mean? *glimpse* (line 2), *last respects* (line 4), *jostling* (line 13), *abide* (line 16), *cholera* (line 37), *hollow laugh* (line 71), *apprentices* (line 94).

Independent Group Task

Word level: *multi-syllabic words* **(20 mins)**

Ask the children to look through the story and to collect five two-syllable words, ten three-syllable words, four four-syllable words (*coronation, interrupted, apprentices, everybody*).

24

Lesson 2

Teaching Objectives

- *to investigate how settings and characters are built up from small details (T1)*
- *to distinguish between the spellings and meanings of common homophones (W6)*

Whole Class Shared Reading

Text level: *setting and character* **(20 mins)**

Reread the story to the class. Ask the children to look carefully through the story and to find words or phrases which describe Beatrice's house. Write these on the board. (*grand, new, edge of park, gate, path, balcony, huge staircase*)

They should then do the same with the character of the apprentice. (*thin, dirty, smelt disgusting, cut on cheek, ragged, unfit, weak*)

Discuss how these descriptions help us to picture the setting and characters.

Word level: *homophones* **(10 mins)**

Explain to the class that homophones are words which sound the same but which have a different spelling and meaning. Write the words *write, right, rite* on the board. Ask the children to look carefully through the story to find further examples of words which have homophones. For example: *been/bean, see/sea, saw/sore, rough/ruff, new/knew, feet/feat, boy/buoy, course/coarse, sew/sow, knot/not.*

Independent Group Task

Text level: *presentation of character* **(20 mins)**

Ask the children to collect words and phrases from the story that help to build up a picture of Olivia's character as a young girl.

Lesson 3

Teaching Objective

- *to revise work on verbs (S2)*

Whole Class Shared Reading

Sentence level: *verb tenses* **(30 mins)**

Look at *Big Book* page 2. This is an excerpt from the story. Ask the children to underline the verbs, including the auxilary verb. Discuss the tense of each one. Point out that the narrative is in the past tense and the speech is in the present tense.

Additional ideas are given for group work without PCMs.

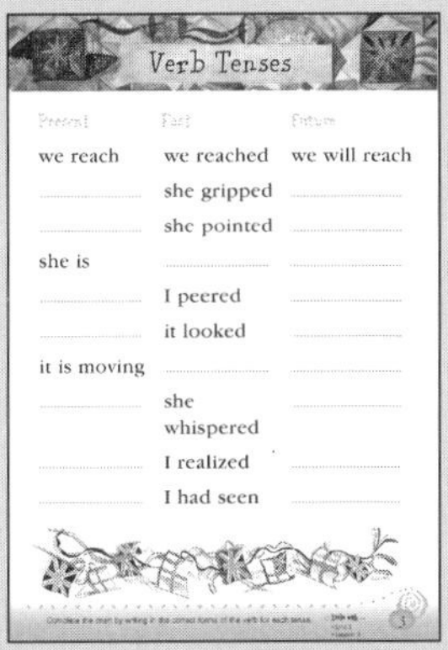

Verb Tenses

Present	Past	Future
we reach	we reached	we will reach
....	she gripped	....
....	she pointed	....
she is	....	....
....	I peered	....
....	it looked	....
it is moving	....	....
....	she whispered	....
....	I realized	....
....	I had seen	....

Lessons link directly to the *Literacy Skills Big Books* and guidance is provided on how to use them.

Reread the passage, stopping at the end of each sentence. Ask the children to tell you how to change the past tense verbs into the present tense each time you pause.

Turn to *Big Book* page 3 which contains a chart identifying the future, the present and the past tenses. Show the children an example of a regular verb (eg *I reached, I reach, I will reach*) and an irregular verb (eg *I was, I am, I will be*). Ask them to help you complete the chart.

Independent Group Task

Sentence level: *verb tenses* **(20 mins)**

Consolidate verb tenses with PCM 1.

Lesson 4

Teaching Objective

- *to explore narrative order (T4)*

Whole Class Shared Reading and Writing

Text level: *narrative order* **(30 mins)**

Look at *Big Book* page 4. This is a completed story frame with the events of the story mapped on to it. Cover the climax and resolution with 'Blu-Tack' and a sheet of paper. Talk to the children about the introduction and the build-up of the story. Then ask them to predict what should go under the climax section. See if their predictions are correct. Talk about the resolution to the story.

Turn to *Big Book* page 5 which contains a story frame for the class to complete. Select either a contemporary story that the class all know or a traditional tale. Ask the children to help you to complete the frame. For example, a chart for *Little Red Riding Hood* might be set out in the following way:

Introduction: starts at home, Granny is sick, Little Red Riding Hood has to take food to her Granny. Warning about not leaving the path.

Build-up: Red Riding Hood meets wolf...

Independent Group Task

Text level: *narrative order* **(20 mins)**

Put the events of a familiar story on to the story frame using PCM 2.

Lesson 5

Teaching Objectives

- *to identify the main characteristics of key characters (T2)*
- *write character sketches focusing on small details (T11)*

Whole Class Shared Reading

Text level: *character details* **(30 mins)**

Ask the children to look back through the story and collect all the details which tell us about the character of Beatrice. For example her reactions towards the boy, her reactions to Mr Soames, how she behaved in the crowd.

Ask children to find textual evidence for the following:

Beatrice was wealthy
she was selfish
she was unsympathetic.

Ask them to find evidence about Olivia to show that she was:

sympathetic to the boy
brave
caring
optimistic.

In what ways were the characters of Olivia and Beatrice different?

Ask the children to think of some adjectives to describe Beatrice and Olivia.

Independent Group Task

Text level: *writing as a character* **(20 mins)**

Complete the diary entries by Beatrice or Olivia using PCM 3a or 3b as appropriate.

25

Name ______________

My Diary by Beatrice

Fill in the diary as though you were Beatrice.

Today I was so excited because ______________

The crowds were so bad that we decided ______________

When we got to my home we saw ______________

I did not like the boy because ______________

When the boy ran off I asked the maid to ______________

Then we ran on to the balcony just in time to see ______________

I hope that I never have to meet ______________

PCM 3a

Teaching objective: Y4 T1 T11 to write character sketches focusing on small details

Links with Unit 1 Lesson 5

PCMs provide group work linked to the whole-class session.

Lessons clearly divided to follow the structure of the Literacy Hour.

Weekly plan for Unit 1: *Not Always a Perfect Place*

National Literacy Strategy Teaching Objectives

Weekly Plan **Not always a Perfect Place by Judy Waite**

Name of school

	Class: Year Group(s): 4 Term: 1 Week Beg: Teacher: Whole class – shared reading and writing	Whole class – phonics, spelling, vocabulary and grammar	* Guided group tasks (reading or writing)	Guided group tasks (reading or writing)	Independent group tasks 5 ability groups: A = high attainers E = low attainers C + D = average B = above average	Plenary
Mon	Read the piece to the class. Ask questions to: • check understanding • explore chronology in narrative.	Extend vocabulary by discussing meaning of difficult words from passage.	Guided Reading/Writing E • Support work in dividing words into syllables. T	T	A • Read first chapter of the story Take a Run and Jump. B • Practise spelling of multi-syllabic words in the text with a partner. C+D • Find multi-syllabic words in the text. OA | OA | OA |	
Tues	Reread the piece focusing on setting and character. Class to find descriptive phrases.	Explain homophones and invite children to find egs., in the piece.	Guided Reading B • Introduce Take a Run and Jump (card 11) and read to page 8. T	T	A • Write a description of Olivia's character on a girl. C, D & E • Collect words and phrases from the text that describe Olivia. OA | OA | OA |	
Wed	Reread text on Big Book page 2 discussing verb tenses. Children to underline verbs.	Using Big Book page 3 model how to change verbs into past, present and future. Ask children to follow your example.	Guided Writing D • Support work on verb tenses. T	T	A+B • Do PCM 1 on verbs and them write sentences independently. C+E • Work on vero tenses using PCM 1. OA | OA | OA |	
Thur	Using Big Book page 4 discuss and explain narrative order in relation to the text. Guided Writing Ask children to identify narrative order of well-known story and write on Big Book page 5.		Guided Reading Take through reading card on Take a Run and Jump (card 11). T	T	B • Plan narrative order of own story. C & E • Identify narrative order of a well-known story using PCM 2. D • PCM 1 on verb tenses. OA | OA | OA |	
Fri	Ask children to scan text to describe the characters with close reference to the text.	Remind children about adjectives by asking for adjectives to describe main characters.	Guided Reading Introduce It's a Hoopoe! (Card 9) and read to page 35. T	T	A+B • Fill in Olivia's diary using PCM 3b. D+E • Fill in Beatrice's diary using PCM 3a OA | OA | OA |	

* We have assumed one guided group task per 20 minutes.

Guided reading and associated group activities

Stage 1 Guided Reading books

At each Stage of Literacy World there are five books specifically written for guided reading. For Stage 2, these books are:

Cheat!	Novel
Raiders!	Novel
Children Behaving Badly	Short stories
Take a Run and Jump	Short stories
The Alien and Other Plays	Plays

These books cover a wide range of the genre recommended by the *Framework* document. We recognize that teachers will want children to read as widely as possible at this level, so we have produced a carefully graded core set of books which will be supplemented by wider reading. For each stage there is a set of Guided Reading cards, written by practising classroom teachers, to help you structure Guided Reading sessions. The cards can be kept with the teacher's copy of the book.

Guided reading and non-fiction

There are also five non-fiction texts available in Literacy World, which are also designed for Guided Reading sessions and have accompanying teacher cards.

How do you run Guided Reading sessions?

Guided Reading involves the teacher working intensively with a small group of children, during which she supports their reading, thinking and talking about a text. We have made the following assumptions about the way that Guided Reading sessions will be run in schools:

- The teacher will have grouped the children according to their reading abilities and needs.
- The texts used in Guided Reading sessions are at the instructional level of the children. An average reader should be able to read the text at a level of 90–95% accuracy.
- The teacher will meet each Guided Reading group once a week.
- Guided Reading sessions will not always be linked to the work done in the shared part of the lesson. (You could, however, develop work on the *Anthology* in a Guided Reading session.)
- The teacher will control the use of the books in these sessions, so that, for example, the children are all up to the same part of the book when they meet with the teacher. If they are not, it may disrupt some of the teaching strategies you may wish to pursue, like developing predictive skills, for example.
- In the junior years, as the books become longer and more complex, some of the reading of the books will take place outside of the Guided Reading session. This reading will still have to be carefully managed so that the children are all up to the same point in the books when they meet with the teacher and the rest of the group for the Guided Reading session.
- Guided Reading sessions will be organized flexibly according to the needs of the children. With some children, you will still be developing basic reading skills whilst with others you will be developing deeper understanding of the text and extending their reading skills.

The Guided Reading cards

Each card starts with a helpful summary – useful for a quick recap of the book, especially when there might be as many as five different books being used in Guided Reading sessions in any one classroom. This is followed by the list of the key teaching objectives that the books cover. These form the basis of the teaching sessions that follow.

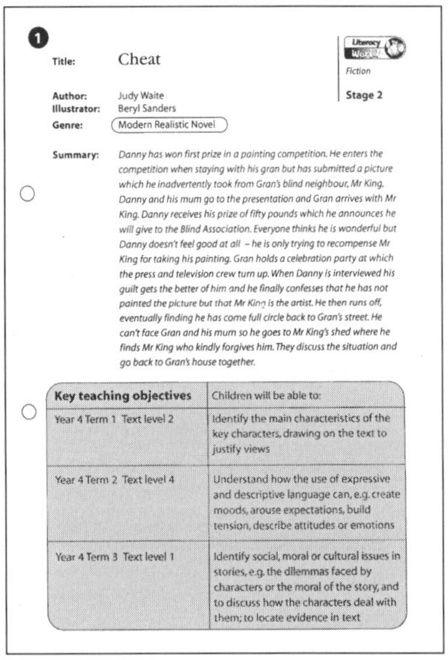

1

Title: Cheat

Fiction

Stage 2

Author: Judy Waite
Illustrator: Beryl Sanders
Genre: Modern Realistic Novel

Summary: *Danny has won first prize in a painting competition. He enters the competition when staying with his gran but has submitted a picture which he inadvertently took from Gran's blind neighbour, Mr King. Danny and his mum go to the presentation and Gran arrives with Mr King. Danny receives his prize of fifty pounds which he announces he will give to the Blind Association. Everyone thinks he is wonderful but Danny doesn't feel good at all – he is only trying to recompense Mr King for taking his painting. Gran holds a celebration party at which the press and television crew turn up. When Danny is interviewed his guilt gets the better of him and he finally confesses that he has not painted the picture but that Mr King is the artist. He then runs off, eventually finding he has come full circle back to Gran's street. He can't face Gran and his mum so he goes to Mr King's shed where he finds Mr King who kindly forgives him. They discuss the situation and go back to Gran's house together.*

Key teaching objectives	Children will be able to:
Year 4 Term 1 Text level 2	Identify the main characteristics of the key characters, drawing on the text to justify views
Year 4 Term 2 Text level 4	Understand how the use of expressive and descriptive language can, e.g. create moods, arouse expectations, build tension, describe attitudes or emotions
Year 4 Term 3 Text level 1	Identify social, moral or cultural issues in stories, e.g. the dilemmas faced by characters or the moral of the story, and to discuss how the characters deal with them; to locate evidence in text

How many Guided Reading sessions will the cards give me?

The Guided Reading cards have been structured in a very flexible way. The teaching units in the guided reading cards usually break down according to the organization of the book, so, for example, in a novel with chapters there will be a teaching unit for every chapter (as well as a before reading and after reading activity for the whole book). For the short stories, the teaching unit will be each story in the book (again, with a before reading and after reading activity for the whole book). The teacher may choose to do a session after every chapter, or combine the sessions once the children have read up to a certain point of the book.

Using the *Reading and Language Skills Books*

The Skills Books are intended to be used by groups who are working independently. They provide a set of activities that follow on from the children's reading. There are, generally, three text, sentence and word level activities for each of the core readers. The activities are broadly differentiated by outcome. Most children should be able to at least attempt the level A questions in the books, but the B and C questions are to be seen as extension activities for more able children. It is not envisaged that children will work through every activity in the *Skills Book*, rather that teachers will select activities from the range offered.

For most of the activities, a copy of the book will be needed as we have tried to develop children's skills of finding evidence from the text for their answers. For some activities, the children will need to have read the whole book. These activities are indicated on the Contents page.

A full breakdown of the teaching objectives covered in the *Skills Book* can be found on page 15 of this Guide.

And finally...

Literacy World also has a complete package for teaching non-fiction skills, with five core texts, *Literacy Lesson Teacher's Guides, Big Books* and Guided Reading cards to support your literacy teaching throughout the junior years.

Coverage of the Framework objectives in the *Reading and Language Skills Book 2*

Activity	Book Pages	NLS Objective
Raiders!		
Words With 'ck	**4**	Y4 T1 W1
Compound Words	**5**	Y4 T3 W11
Replacing 'said'	**6**	Y4 T2 W9
Nouns	**7**	Y4 T2 S1
Apostrophes	**8**	Y4 T2 S2
Verbs	**9**	Y4 T1 S2
Comprehension	**10**	Y4 T1 T1
What Would You Do?	**11**	Y4 T1 T12
Make it More Interesting	**12**	Y4 T2 T13
Cheat!		
Double 'ss'	**13**	Y4 T3 W5
Words Ending in 'ful'	**14**	Y4 T3 W8
Adjectives Ending in 'ible'	**15**	Y4 T3 W9
Commas Show a Pause	**16**	Y4 T1 S5
Commas in Lists	**17**	Y4 T1 S5
Semi-colons in Lists	**18**	Y4 T3 S2
Building up Ideas	**19**	Y4 T3 T3
Danny's Problems	**20**	Y4 T3 T1
Mood, Atmosphere, Emotions	**21**	Y4 T2 T4
Take a Run and Jump and Other Stories		
Words With 'ar'	**22**	Y4 T3 W6
Questions	**23**	Y4 T3 S3
Unfold the Story	**24**	Y4 T3 T3
Letter Strings	**25**	Y4 T3 W3
Change the Order	**26**	Y4 T2 S3
Friendship	**27**	Y4 T3 T1
Adverbs – 'ly'	**28**	Y4 T1 S4
Link the Sentences	**29**	Y4 T3 S4
Exploring Ideas	**30**	Y4 T3 T11
Children Behaving Badly		
Hyphens	**31**	Y4 T3 S2
What Do You Think of Tom?	**32**	Y4 T3 T8
Word Search	**33**	Y4 T3 W6
Speech Marks	**34**	Y4 T3 S2
What Could Sanjay Do?	**35**	Y4 T3 T12
It's a Hoopoe! Listen to its Funny Call	**36**	Y4 T3 W10
What Simon Did	**37**	Y4 T2 T2
Adjectives Ending in 'able'	**38**	Y4 T2 W13
Positive and Negative	**39**	Y4 T3 S3
The Alien and Other Plays		
A Huge Green Alien	**40**	Y4 T2 S1
Character Study	**41**	Y4 T1 T2
Doubles	**42**	Y4 T1 W5
Follow the Pattern	**43**	Y4 T1 T4
Dictionary Work	**44**	Y4 T1 W12
Imagine You Are Tom	**45**	Y4 T1 T2
The Right Word	**46**	Y4 T1 W6
Powerful Verbs	**47**	Y4 T1 S3
Character Sketch	**48**	Y4 T1 T11

Year 4
Term 1

Please note

Due to shortage of space we have included only a basic paraphrase of the Teaching Objective descriptions.

Blocked off Teaching Objectives are ongoing tasks, not for specific unit coverage, or tasks more suitable for non-fiction.

	UNIT 1 historical story	UNIT 1 • PCMs	UNIT 2 historical novel	UNIT 2 • PCMs	UNIT 3 historical playscript	UNIT 3 • PCMs	UNIT 4 historical novel	UNIT 4 • PCMs	UNIT 5 poems based on a common theme	UNIT 5 • PCMs	UNIT 6 poems based on a common theme	UNIT 6 • PCMs
Text level work												
T1 building up settings and characters	✔		✔				✔	✔				
T2 characteristics of key characters	✔											
T3 chronology in narrative	✔		✔									
T4 narrative order	✔	✔					✔					
T5 prepare and perform playscripts					✔	✔						
T6 chart the build-up of a play scene					✔							
T7 compare and contrast poems on similar themes									✔		✔	✔
T8 find out more about popular authors												
T9 different ways of planning stories							✔				✔	
T10 plan story, identifying stages			✔									
T11 write character sketches	✔	✔					✔					
T12 link own experience to historical stories			✔	✔								
T13 write playscripts					✔	✔						
T14 write poems									✔	✔	✔	✔
T15 use paragraphs to organize and sequence writing			✔									
Sentence level work												
S1 check own writing												
S2 revise verbs and verb tenses	✔	✔					✔	✔			✔	
S3 'powerful' verbs			✔	✔							✔	
S4 adverbs			✔	✔	✔							
S5 commas: link with editing and revising own writing					✔	✔	✔					
Word level work												
W1 reading and spelling	✔											
W2 identify mis-spelt words												
W3 independent spelling strategies									✔			
W4 practise new spellings												
W5 spell 2-syllable words with double consonants			✔									
W6 common homophones	✔											
W7 spell regular verb endings					✔							
W8 spell irregular tense changes												
W9 suffixes: -al, -ary, -ic, -ship, -hood, -ness, -ment							✔					
W10 read and spell words in Appendix List 2												
W11 define familiar vocabulary												
W12 alphabetical order							✔	✔				
W13 use rhyming dictionary												
W14 suffixes that make nouns and adjectives into verbs												

Year 4
Term 2

Please note

Due to shortage of space we have included only a basic paraphrase of the Teaching Objective descriptions.

Blocked off Teaching Objectives are ongoing tasks, not for specific unit coverage, or tasks more suitable for non-fiction.

	UNIT 1 novel about imagined world: sci-fi	UNIT 1 • PCMs	UNIT 2 novel about imagined world: sci-fi	UNIT 2 • PCMs	UNIT 3 classic poems	UNIT 3 • PCMs	UNIT 4 novel about imagined world: fantasy adventure	UNIT 4 • PCMs	UNIT 5 modern poem; poem from another culture	UNIT 5 • PCMs	UNIT 6 novel about imagined world: fantasy adventure	UNIT 6 • PCMs
Text level work												
T1 how writers create imaginary worlds	✔										✔	
T2 how settings influence events and affect characters			✔								✔	
T3 compare and contrast settings	✔		✔									
T4 expressive and descriptive language			✔						✔	✔		
T5 figurative language in poetry and prose					✔			✔	✔			
T6 recognizing older poems					✔							
T7 different patterns of rhyme and verse					✔	✔	✔		✔			
T8 review a range of stories												
T9 texts targeted at particular readers	✔	✔										
T10 develop settings in own writing			✔									
T11 write poetry based on poems read					✔				✔			
T12 collaborating to write stories in chapters	✔											
T13 descriptive, expressive language based on reading							✔					✔
T14 notemaking and editing			✔								✔	
Sentence level work												
S1 revise and extend knowledge of adjectives	✔	✔					✔		✔	✔	✔	
S2 use apostrophe to mark possession			✔	✔							✔	✔
S3 significance of word order					✔	✔						
S4 commas, connectives and full stops			✔								✔	
Word level work												
W1 reading and spelling												
W2 identify mis-spelt words												
W3 independent spelling strategies												
W4 practise new spellings												
W5 adding suffix to words ending in -f	✔											
W6 spell words with common endings							✔					
W7 recognize and spell prefixes											✔	
W8 read and spell words in Appendix List 2												
W9 use alternative words and expressions			✔	✔			✔					
W10 words that imply gender												
W11 archaic vocabulary	✔				✔							
W12 define familiar words within constraints	✔	✔										
W13 suffixes that make nouns and verbs into adjectives							✔	✔				

Year 4
Term 3

Please note

Due to shortage of space we have included only a basic paraphrase of the Teaching Objective descriptions.

Blocked off Teaching Objectives are ongoing tasks, not for specific unit coverage, or tasks more suitable for non-fiction.

	UNIT 1 story from another culture	UNIT 1 • PCMs	UNIT 2 novels by the same author	UNIT 2 • PCMs	UNIT 3 novel that raises issues	UNIT 3 • PCMs	UNIT 4 poems in different forms	UNIT 4 • PCMs	UNIT 5 poems in different forms	UNIT 5 • PCMs	UNIT 6 poems in different forms	UNIT 6 • PCMs
Text level work												
T1 social, moral, cultural issues in stories	✔		✔	✔	✔	✔						
T2 stories from other cultures	✔											
T3 use of paragraphs or chapters to structure ideas			✔		✔							
T4 poetry terms and vocabulary							✔		✔		✔	
T5 clap out and count syllables							✔					
T6 the use of rhyme; patterns of rhyme							✔		✔			
T7 simple forms of poetry and their uses							✔		✔		✔	
T8 critical evaluation	✔		✔		✔							
T9 in-depth reading and analysis of an author's work			✔									
T10 describe, review and widen own reading												
T11 explore main issues through writing	✔	✔	✔	✔	✔							
T12 alternative ending for known story	✔											
T13 write longer stories in chapters from plans												
T14 poems with different styles and structures							✔	✔	✔	✔	✔	✔
T15 polished poetry through revision									✔		✔	
Sentence level work												
S1 grammar to identify words that can be changed	✔	✔										
S2 common punctuation marks			✔	✔					✔			
S3 how grammar alters according to sentence type	✔				✔							
S4 the use of connectives												
Word level work												
W1 reading and spelling												
W2 identify mis-spelt words												
W3 independent spelling strategies							✔				✔	
W4 practise new spellings												
W5 the occurrence of certain letters within words												
W6 words with common letter strings, different pronunciations	✔	✔										
W7 words with common roots			✔						✔	✔		
W8 extend and compound words through adding parts							✔	✔			✔	✔
W9 suffixes: -ible, -able, -ive, -tion, -sion					✔	✔						
W10 distinguish between apostrophe for possession or contraction			✔									
W11 spelling compound words					✔							
W12 diminutives					✔							

Literacy World and the Northern Ireland Curriculum

The following chart shows how Literacy World meets the programme of study for Key Stage 2 English in Northern Ireland. The Speaking and Listening Attainment Target has not been specifically included on this chart, but Literacy World encourages oral communication in its Shared and Guided Reading components.

Reading

Context and Audience: The Guided Reading strand of Literacy World offers opportunities for reading individually, to the teacher and in groups. The Shared Reading Strand, based on the *Anthologies*, is designed for class reading and offers some reading in pairs.

Range: The Shared Reading strand of Literacy World offers a range of different fiction genres and poems. It also encourages reading of own and others' work. Literacy World's non-fiction strand offers a whole range of non-fiction texts, including dictionaries and encyclopedias.

Purpose: Literacy World encourages independent reading for own enjoyment by providing good quality fiction. The Guided Reading books and *Anthologies* contain texts from varied cultures, traditions and beliefs helping children to learn about themselves and others, and the non-fiction provides practice in locating information as well as cross-curricular material.

Activities: The Shared Reading lesson plans and Guided Reading cards offer strategies for helping children understand texts. They focus on distinctive features of a text, encourage reading aloud with inflection, contain activities on representing texts in different visual forms, and consistently encourage expression of own opinion with reference to the text. Several units of the Shared Reading, Stage 1 particularly, look at manipulating language. Texts are revisited after initial reading encouraging children to review initial response. Features of language are comprehensively covered in the *Reading and Language Skills Books,* the *Big Books* and in the Shared Reading lesson plans.

Expected Outcomes: Shared Reading lesson plans and the Guided Reading cards encourage sensitive response to texts and writers' intentions are discussed. The non-fiction strand demands use of organizational information, deals with how different media present information and teaches understanding of different reading skills. The Shared Reading lesson plans include work on placing readers in the position of characters and on predicting texts. There are many opportunities for children to model their own writing on texts read as well as some tasks on writing for different audiences.

Writing

Planning: planning is encouraged in the Shared Reading lesson plans, modelled by the teacher in the *Big Book* and supported by PCMs. It includes discussion, brainstorming ideas, making notes and preparing outlines.

Purpose: The Shared Reading lesson plans provide scope to write thoughts, feelings and imaginings, to describe, narrate and express a point of view. The non-fiction strand demands reporting, persuading, interpreting of data and giving instructions.

Context and Audience: writing arises mainly from responses to reading. Children are encouraged to consider audience in their writing and some specific work is done on adapting text for different audiences.

Range: Literacy World offers opportunities to write stories, diaries, poems (including experimenting with rhyme, rhythm, verses, verbal play and dialect), notes, descriptions, dialogues. Discussions of differences between spoken and written language are covered particularly at Stages 1 and 3. Use of punctuation marks for writing is covered comprehensively in the Shared Reading lesson plans, including the PCMs and the *Reading and Language Skills Books.* The non-fiction strand offers writing of reports, instructions and notes, as well as discussions about layout and use of alphabet.

Expected Outcomes: Literacy World teaches children to use expressive language in writing. This is modelled in the *Big Books* and specific tasks are offered in the PCMs. Teaching of structure is given in the form of *Big Book* and PCM plans and models. There is comprehensive coverage of punctuation and grammar to enable children to use paragraphs, use grammatical terms, understand conventions of grammar, connectives and pronouns, set out and punctuate direct speech. Spelling strategies are also encouraged generally, and specifically provided on problematic words.

Literacy World and the Scottish 5–14 Guidelines

The following charts show where, in Stages 1 and 2 of Literacy World, you can use the most appropriate components for meeting the Level B and C Attainment Targets (ATs). The reading and writing strands of the Scottish Guidelines are interwoven throughout the fiction and non-fiction teaching units in Literacy World. Literacy World takes as its starting point the teaching of genre through a range of examples in the *Essential Texts Anthologies*. In doing this, the writer's ideas and craft are continually looked at. From this starting point the specific grammar and vocabulary work is taught. To find specific examples of genre coverage, refer to the chart on pages 4–5 of this *Guide*. To find where specific organizational and language features, grammatical terms and spelling and vocabulary skills are taught, refer to the NLS *Framework* correlation charts on pages 16–18 of this *Guide*.

Writing strand	Level B	Level C	Components in Literacy World
Functional writing	Write briefly in an appropriate form for a variety of practical purposes.	Write in an appropriate form and with adequate vocabulary to communicate key events, facts or ideas.	Photocopiable writing frames in the Stages 1 and 2 non-fiction *Teacher's Guides* help support children's functional writing. PCMs in this guide and text level activities in the *Reading and Language Skills Books* also provide opportunities for this.
Personal writing	Write briefly and in an appropriate sequence about a personal experience, giving an indication of feelings, using adequate vocabulary.	Write about a personal experience for a specific purpose and audience, using appropriate organization and vocabulary.	Practice in writing personal recounts can be found in the non-fiction PCMs; opportunities are also provided throughout the fiction PCMs for personal writing.
Imaginative writing	Write a brief, imaginative story or poem or dialogue, with discernible organization and using adequate vocabulary.	Write a brief, imaginative story, poem or play, using appropriate organization and vocabulary.	Writing frames to enable children to write poems, narratives and plays can be found throughout the PCMs in the Stages 1 and 2 fiction *Teacher's Guides*. Opportunities for leading shared writing sessions can be found in the Stages 1 and 2 fiction *Literacy Skills Big Books*.
Punctuation and structure	Use capital letters and full stops correctly in more than one sentence, and use common linking words: and, but, then, so, that.	Punctuate many sentences accurately; Simple use of commas; Simple use of question marks. Begin to use paragraphs to structure writing.	The PCMs in this *Guide*, offer ample practice in the use of these skills. Also the *Reading and Language Skills Books* reinforce this practice. Within the teaching of non-fiction, the use of connectives is a strong feature.

Writing strand	Level B	Level C	Components in Literacy World
Knowledge about language	Show that they know, understand and can use at least the following terms: *Letter; Sentence; Word; Planning; Capital; Drafting; Full stop; Re-drafting.*	Show that they know, understand and can use the following terms: *Noun; Purpose; Verb; Audience. Comma; Question mark;*	The PCMs in this *Guide*, and at Stage 2, offer ample practice in the use of these skills. Also the *Reading and Language Skills Books* reinforce this practice. Planning, drafting and redrafting is strongly developed in the shared writing strand of the non-fiction lesson plans.
Reading strand			
Reading for information	Find and use, with teacher support, information specific to their needs from a range of information and reference sources.	Find and use information specific to their needs from a range of informational and reference sources.	All the non-fiction information books at Stages 1 and 2; teacher-led demonstration of these skills through the Stages 1 and 2 non-fiction *Literacy Skills Big Books* and the Stages 1 and 2 non-fiction *Literacy Lesson Teacher's Guides*.
Reading for enjoyment	Read stories, poems and informational texts regularly for enjoyment.	Read regularly for enjoyment and give an opinion on texts of different kinds.	Stages 1 and 2 Guided Reading books. Teacher-led discussion through the use of the *Guided Reading Teacher's Cards* which accompany each text.
Reading to reflect on the writer's ideas and craft	Read straightforward texts, and in discussion and writing show that they understand the main ideas.	Read a variety of straightforward texts, and in discussion and writing show that they understand the main and supporting ideas, and can draw conclusions from the text where appropriate.	Every piece in the Stages 1 and 2 *Essential Texts* anthologies can be used to fulfil this AT. Lesson plans for teachers to lead this work can be found in the Stages 1 and 2 fiction *Literacy Lesson Teacher's Guides*, which provide detailed notes.
Awareness of genre	Show recognition of a few features of different types of simple texts: stories, poems, dramatic texts, informational and reference texts.	Identify a few obvious features of form and content in different types of text: stories, poems, dramatic texts, newspaper items, informational and reference texts.	The genre coverage for the *Essential Texts* can be found on pages 4–5 of this *Guide*. The non-fiction books have been written as models of non-fiction genre. In addition the non-fiction *Literacy Lesson Teacher's Guide* introduces each non-fiction genre with a model text, with full guidance on how to teach it.
Knowledge about language	Show that they know, understand and can use at least the following terms: *Author; Title; Chapter; Index; Contents; Character; Setting the scene; Poem; Dictionary; Question mark.*	Show that they know, understand and can use the following terms: *Fiction; Non-fiction; Thesaurus; Reference book; Plot; Dialogue; Main character; Conflict; Verse; Paragraph; Headline; Speech marks; Exclamation mark.*	The detailed breakdown of the NLS objective coverage on pages 16–18 of this *Guide* will show you where these specific language features are covered in the teaching units, and practised in the PCMs. Further practice in the use of these features can be found in the *Reading and Language Skills Books*, which can be used alongside the Guided Reading books. The non-fiction features will be found in the Stages 1 and 2 non-fiction *Literacy Lesson Teacher's Guides*.

Year 4 • Term 1: Literature Overview

Introduction

The range of texts for this term has three strands: historical stories and short novels; play scripts; and poems based on common themes. The *Anthology* has been organized to start with the more accessible texts and to move on to more challenging prose and poetry as the term progresses. The poetry has been grouped together to be studied at end of term, since this is easier to accommodate with all the other end of term activities.

The first unit is **Not Always a Perfect Place** by Judy Waite. Judy Waite writes for children of all ages and a full length novel *Cheat!* is published in the Literacy World Guided Readers. This short historical story paints a vivid picture of the contrast between the well-to-do and the poor of Victorian England. The rights and wrongs of this situation are not completely clear cut. A young boy describes his hard life as a factory worker. However the factory overseer argues that life for the poor has improved since he was a lad and the world is not a 'perfect place'. This is an excellent introduction to historical novels and how they manage to create the atmosphere of the period.

Raiders! by Lynne Benton is an extract taken from the full-length novel which forms part of the Literacy World's Guided Readers. Lynne Benton is a primary school teacher and mother of four children. In this story, young Jack Watson goes through a time-slip and finds himself a member of an Anglo-Saxon family back in the time of the Viking raids. The raiders attack the village and Jack fights with his father to save them. The story is action-packed, and provides a good contrast to the first unit. Readers will learn how a time-slip works, and how settings and characters can be built up from small details. The pace of the story fluctuates; some events are skimmed over very quickly, whilst others are described in greater detail.

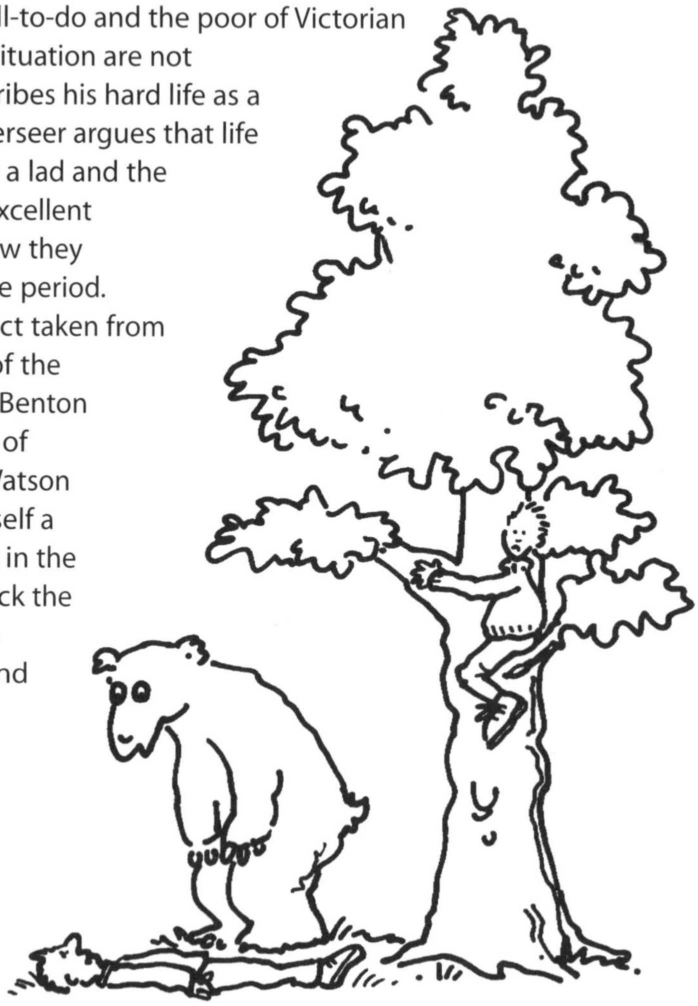

A Jumble for the Queen by Julia Donaldson is an historical play set in the time of Queen Elizabeth I. These five short scenes give the class a glimpse of the kind of life girls and boys could expect in the sixteenth century. Joan works long hours in the kitchens of Sir Richard Ash's house, whilst her brother Thomas is threatened with a beating at his school. This unit meets the demands of the National Literacy Strategy by providing a clear example of how to set scenes and create storylines which the children can then follow when writing their own playscripts.

The extract from **The Stove Haunting** by the famous children's author Bel Mooney is a very powerful and demanding piece of writing. Daniel (who has time-slipped back into 1838) is taken to visit a family living in extreme poverty. The scene is described in minute detail, and creates an image that remains with the reader for a long time. This story is an excellent example of how settings and characters can be built up from small details.

The four poems that conclude this term's work are based on two themes: Family and Winter. These are supplemented by two further poems from the *Big Book*; **My Gran** and **Sir Winter**. The family collection spans the age range, beginning with early childhood in **Family Photo Album**, and ending with a wonderful poem about **My Grandpa** by the teacher-turned poet, Ian Souter. The winter theme consists of the famous poem **Something Told the Wild Geese** by the American poet, Rachel Field, and **Snow Spell** by Berlie Doherty. These poems are very different in style and sentiment, and make a good contrast for the class to explore.

Unit 1

Not Always a Perfect Place

Range: historical story

Learning Outcomes:

Text level: investigating settings and characters; exploring story chronology; narrative order; main characteristics of key characters; writing character sketches

Sentence level: investigating verb tenses

Word level: multi-syllabic words; homophones

Lesson 1

Teaching Objectives

- *to explore chronology (T3)*
- *identifying syllabic patterns in multi-syllabic words (W1)*

Whole Class Shared Reading

Text level: *story chronology* **(20 mins)**

Read the story to the class. Ask the following questions:

- Where was Olivia at the opening of the story?
- Where was Olivia at the end of the story?
- Why did the story open and end at the same place?
- What do we call it when stories move from one time to events in the past? (*time slip, flashback*)
- What has Olivia waited sixty years to see?
- Who was the man with the scar on his face?
- What must have happened in the sixty years since Olivia first saw him?
- Do you think Olivia spoke to the man with the scar?
- Why did Soames say '*The world is not always a perfect place?*'

Word level: *less familiar vocabulary* **(10 mins)**

Ask the children what they think the following mean? *glimpse* (line 2), *last respects* (line 4), *jostling* (line 13), *abide* (line 16), *cholera* (line 37), *hollow laugh* (line 71), *apprentices* (line 94).

Independent Group Task

Word level: *multi-syllabic words* **(20 mins)**

Ask the children to look through the story and to collect five two-syllable words, ten three-syllable words, four four-syllable words (*coronation, interrupted, apprentices, everybody*).

Lesson 2

Teaching Objectives

- *to investigate how settings and characters are built up from small details (T1)*
- *to distinguish between the spellings and meanings of common homophones (W6)*

Whole Class Shared Reading

Text level: *setting and character* **(20 mins)**

Reread the story to the class. Ask the children to look carefully through the story and to find words or phrases which describe Beatrice's house. Write these on the board. (*grand, new, edge of park, gate, path, balcony, huge staircase*)

They should then do the same with the character of the apprentice. (*thin, dirty, smelt disgusting, cut on cheek, ragged, unfit, weak*)

Discuss how these descriptions help us to picture the setting and characters.

Word level: *homophones* **(10 mins)**

Explain to the class that homophones are words which sound the same but which have a different spelling and meaning. Write the words *write, right, rite* on the board. Ask the children to look carefully through the story to find further examples of words which have homophones. For example: *been/bean, see/sea, saw/sore, rough/ruff, new/knew, feet/feat, boy/buoy, course/coarse, sew/sow, knot/not.*

Independent Group Task

Text level: *presentation of character* **(20 mins)**

Ask the children to collect words and phrases from the story that help to build up a picture of Olivia's character as a young girl.

Lesson 3

Teaching Objective

- *to revise work on verbs (S2)*

Whole Class Shared Reading

Sentence level: *verb tenses* **(30 mins)**

Look at *Big Book* page 2. This is an excerpt from the story. Ask the children to underline the verbs, including the auxilary verb. Discuss the tense of each one. Point out that the narrative is in the past tense and the speech is in the present tense.

Reread the passage, stopping at the end of each sentence. Ask the children to tell you how to change the past tense verbs into the present tense each time you pause.

Turn to *Big Book* page 3 which contains a chart identifying the future, the present and the past tenses. Show the children an example of a regular verb (eg *I reached, I reach, I will reach*) and an irregular verb (eg *I was, I am, I will be*). Ask them to help you complete the chart.

Independent Group Task

Sentence level: *verb tenses* **(20 mins)**

Consolidate verb tenses with PCM 1.

Lesson 4

Teaching Objective

- *to explore narrative order (T4)*

Whole Class Shared Reading and Writing

Text level: *narrative order* **(30 mins)**

Look at *Big Book* page 4. This is a completed story frame with the events of the story mapped on to it. Cover the climax and resolution with 'Blu-Tack' and a sheet of paper. Talk to the children about the introduction and the build-up of the story. Then ask them to predict what should go under the climax section. See if their predictions are correct. Talk about the resolution to the story.

Turn to *Big Book* page 5 which contains a story frame for the class to complete. Select either a contemporary story that the class all know or a traditional tale. Ask the children to help you to complete the frame. For example, a chart for *Little Red Riding Hood* might be set out in the following way:
Introduction: starts at home, Granny is sick, Little Red Riding Hood has to take food to her Granny. Warning about not leaving the path.
Build-up: Red Riding Hood meets wolf...

Independent Group Task

Text level: *narrative order* **(20 mins)**

Put the events of a familiar story on to the story frame using PCM 2.

Lesson 5

Teaching Objectives

- *to identify the main characteristics of key characters (T2)*
- *write character sketches focusing on small details (T11)*

Whole Class Shared Reading

Text level: *character details* **(30 mins)**

Ask the children to look back through the story and collect all the details which tell us about the character of Beatrice. For example her reactions towards the boy, her reactions to Mr Soames, how she behaved in the crowd.

Ask children to find textual evidence for the following:

Beatrice was wealthy
she was selfish
she was unsympathetic.

Ask them to find evidence about Olivia to show that she was:

sympathetic to the boy
brave
caring
optimistic.

In what ways were the characters of Olivia and Beatrice different?

Ask the children to think of some adjectives to describe Beatrice and Olivia.

Independent Group Task

Text level: *writing as a character* **(20 mins)**

Complete the diary entries by Beatrice or Olivia using PCM 3a or 3b as appropriate.

Name ____________________

Verb Tenses

Underline the verbs in the sentences. Then write what tense they are in on the lines provided – present, past or future tense.

I went to the shops. __________ tense

He works in the factory. __________ tense

They walked to the beach. __________ tense

She will go to school tomorrow. __________ tense

They will be tired soon. __________ tense

I call out to the dog. __________ tense

My horse will jump that fence soon. __________ tense

He reads the paper. __________ tense

I carried the box home. __________ tense

She is wearing a blue shirt. __________ tense

Teaching objective: *Y4 T1 S2 to revise work on verbs*
Links with **Unit 1 Lesson 3**

Name ____________________

Story Frame

Choose a story you know well and put the events in order under the appropriate headings below.

Title ____________________

Introduction

____

____

____

Build-up

____

____

____

Climax or conflict

____

____

____

Resolution

____

____

____

Teaching objective: *Y4 T1 T4 to explore narrative order*
Links with **Unit 1 Lesson 4**

Name ____________________

My Diary by Beatrice

Fill in the diary as though you were Beatrice.

Today I was so excited because ____________________

____

The crowds were so bad that we decided ____________________

____

When we got to my home we saw ____________________

____

I did not like the boy because ____________________

____

When the boy ran off I asked the maid to ____________________

____

Then we ran on to the balcony just in time to see ____________________

____

I hope that I never have to meet ____________________

____

Teaching objective: *Y4 T1 T11 to write character sketches focusing on small details*

Links with **Unit 1 Lesson 5**

Name ______________________________

My Diary by Olivia

Fill in the diary as though you were Olivia.

I was so excited today because ______________________________

____

The crowds were so bad that ______________________________

____

When we got to Beatrice's house we saw ______________________________

____

I was not afraid of the boy and ______________________________

____

When the overseer came I ______________________________

____

I think that ______________________________

____

I hope that ______________________________

____

Teaching objective: *Y4 T1 T11 to write character sketches focusing on small details*
Links with **Unit 1 Lesson 5**

Unit 2

Raiders!

Range: historical novel

Learning Outcomes:

Text level: investigating settings and characters; exploring chronology in narrative; to write independently linking own experience to situations in historical stories; to plan a story; paragraphing

Sentence level: identifying the use of powerful verbs; identifying adverbs and their function in sentences

Word level: spelling two-syllable words containing double consonants

Lesson 1

Teaching Objectives

- *story recall and response to text*
- *identify the use of powerful verbs (S3)*

Whole Class Shared Reading

Text level: *response to story* **(20 mins)**

Read the excerpt from this historical novel to the class and ask the following questions:

- What is the boy's name in contemporary time?
- Who are the Raiders?
- Describe their boats.
- What do the raiders do when the boat lands?
- What does Edric do?
- What happens when the Raiders reach the village?
- How does his father save Edric?
- How does Edric save his father?
- What do you think happens next?

Sentence level: *powerful verbs* **(10 mins)**

Remind the children that verbs are the action words within sentences. Look at lines 35–44. Ask the children to identify the verbs. Write them on the board and discuss how the choice of verbs helps to convey the drama of the situation: *wriggle, leap, skim, pounding, warn, bar, race, bang.*

Independent Group Task

Sentence level: *powerful verbs* **(20 mins)**

Choose the right powerful verbs using PCM 1.

Lesson 2

Teaching Objectives

- *to explore chronology in narrative (T3)*
- *to investigate how characters are built up from small details (T1)*

Whole Class Shared Reading

Text level: *exploring chronology* **(30 mins)**

Reread the extract to the class. Ask the class to look at *Big Book* page 6. This is a breakdown of simultaneous events in the chronology of the story. Ask the children to help you to sort out who was doing what, when. Write the answers succinctly on the acetate sheet.

Ask the children to devise questions for each other that can be answered from the completed chart, eg *What was father doing when Edric was collecting firewood?*

Independent Group Task

Text level work: *presentation of characters* **(20 mins)**

From the excerpt collect 10 words or phrases that suggest the characters are frightened. For example *'mouth goes dry', 'too terrified to move', 'menacing', 'I am horribly afraid'.*

Lesson 3

Teaching Objectives

- *to investigate how characters are built up from small details (T1)*
- *to write independently linking own experiences to situations in historical stories (T12)*
- *to spell two-syllable words containing double consonants (W5)*

Whole Class Shared Reading

Text level: *investigating character* **(20 mins)**

Ask the children to search through the story to find any descriptive details that help us to understand the characters of Edric and his father. Write the evidence on the board.

For example *Edric = forgetful* (line 6), *frightened* (line 13), *practical* (line 14), *fast runner* (line 37), *brave* (line 75), *angry* (line 101), *quick thinking* (line 101).

Finally, ask the children to suggest three adjectives that sum up Edric and three more adjectives that sum up his father. For example Edric's father = *fearless, fierce*, etc.

Word level: *two-syllable words with double consonants* **(10 mins)**

Turn to *Big Book* page 7 and read aloud the words taken from the story emphasizing the two syllables. Point out how the syllabic break comes after the double consonant, eg *hudd-le, litt-le.*

Ask the children to tell you how to break the remaining words and write their answers on the acetate sheet in the *Big Book*. Give the children a few minutes then test the spelling of the words.

Finally, ask them to think of further words that conform to this pattern. You might like to give clues. For example, *how a horse runs (gallop), the way a duck walks (waddle).* You could provide clues for the following: *sorrow, marry, flutter, matter, written, current, narrow, common, correct.*

Independent Group Task

Text level: *personal response to story* **(20 mins)**

Using PCM 2, think about what you would do if you were in the character's situation.

Lesson 4

Teaching Objective

- *to identify adverbs and understand their functions in sentences (S4)*

Whole Class Shared Reading

Sentence level: *verbs and adverbs* **(30 mins)**

Turn to *Big Book* page 8, read out the sentences and ask the class to identify the verbs. Underline these in red. Then ask them to identify the adverbs which describe the verbs. Underline these in blue.

Turn to the chart on *Big Book* page 9. Ask the children to suggest two adverbs that could describe the verbs, and a further adverb to answer the questions.

Independent Group Task

Sentence level: *adverbs* **(20 mins)**

Identify and correct the adverbs using PCM 3a or 3b as appropriate.

Lesson 5

Teaching Objectives

- *to plan a story identifying the stages of its telling (T10)*
- *using paragraphing in story writing to organize and sequence the narrative (T15)*

Whole Class Shared Writing

Text level: *planning events in story* **(30 mins)**

Reread the last page of *Raiders!* and ask the children to draw out all the clues that will help them to predict what happens next; for example: *the roof is alight, the Viking is stunned, Father is wounded, Edric is unconscious.* Ask the children to help you to plan the events of the next chapter. Make brief notes of their suggestions on the board.

- What has happened to Edric?
- What does father do?
- Does Elfreda come back into the story?
- How will this chapter end?

Discuss with the children how the answers to each question will form different stages in the narrative and will therefore require separate paragraphs. Talk to the children about how linked ideas are put together in one paragraph. When a new set of ideas is introduced we start a new paragraph.

Independent Group Task

Text level: *writing from the point of view of a character* **(20 mins)**

Ask the children to write a paragraph entitled *'What would I do next?'* They should write from either Edric's or Elfreda's point of view.

Name ______________________

Powerful Verbs

Fill in the gaps with the correct powerful verbs.

yelled flung attack whirled sliced crept defended staggered

The raiders __________ towards the village.

They used axes to __________ the gate.

The raiders __________ terrible bloodcurdling cries.

The villagers __________ themselves with swords and sticks.

The raider __________ his axe around his head.

The axe __________ Edric's father's sword in two.

Edric __________ the wooden swallow at the raider.

The raider __________ back and dropped the axe.

***Now write two sentences using the following verbs:* chased, fought.**

____

____

____

____

Teaching objective: *Y4 T1 S3 identify the use of powerful verbs*
Links with **Unit 2 Lesson 1**

Name ______________________

Literacy World

Viking Adventure!

What would you have done in the following situations?

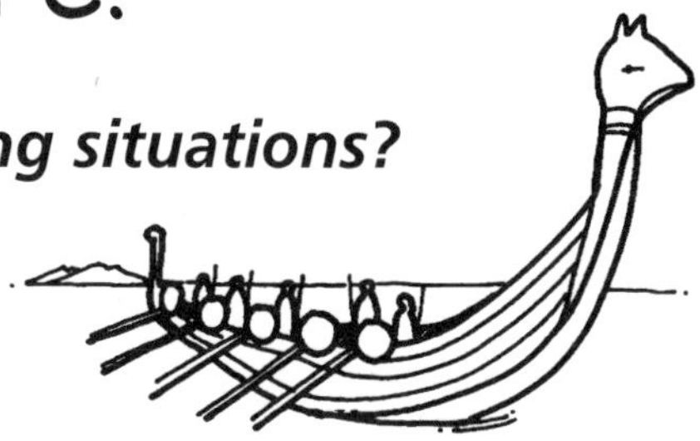

1 When you first saw the raiders arriving?

____

____

____

2 When you got to the village?

____

____

____

3 When the Viking grabbed you?

____

____

____

4 When father is wounded?

____

____

____

Teaching objective: *Y5 T1 T12 to write independently, linking own experiences to situations in historical stories*

Links with **Unit 2 Lesson 3**

Name ____________________

Literacy World

What's Wrong?

Circle the incorrect word and write the sentence correctly underneath.

1 The snail moved slow down the path.

____

2 The car sped swift away.

____

3 She went quick to the shops.

____

4 He spoke loud on the telephone.

____

5 They did their homework careful.

____

6 He scored the goal perfect.

____

Teaching objective: *Y4 T1 S4 to identify adverbs and understand their functions in sentences*

Links with **Unit 2 Lesson 4**

Name ______________________

Verb and Adverb Hunt

Circle the verbs and underline the adverbs.
Write a sentence of your own for each adverb.

1 The snail moved slowly down the path.

____

2 The car sped swiftly away.

____

3 She went quickly to the shops.

____

4 He spoke loudly on the telephone.

____

5 They did their homework carefully.

____

6 He scored the goal perfectly.

____

Teaching objective: *Y4 T1 S4 to identify adverbs and understand their functions in sentences*
Links with **Unit 2 Lesson 4**

Unit 3

A Jumble for the Queen

Range: historical playscript

Learning Outcomes:

Text level: to prepare, read and perform playscripts; to chart the build-up of a play scene; to write a playscript

Sentence level: using commas to mark grammatical boundaries within sentences; adverbs

Word level: to spell regular verb endings

Lesson 1

Teaching Objectives

- *to prepare, read and perform playscripts (T5)*
- *to explore meanings of words and phrases from Elizabethan times*

Whole Class Shared Reading

Text level: *performing and responding to a play* **(20 mins)**

Ask six children to read the parts of the characters in the play. Ask the following questions:

Scene 1
- What event are the cooks preparing for?
- What food is being prepared?
- Why is the pastry cook cross with Joan?

Scene 2
- Why was Tom late for school?
- What might happen to him?

Scene 3
- What is the Queen taking on her visit to Kent?

Scene 4
- Why is Percival cross this time?
- How do you make tooth soap?

Scene 5
- Why is the Master cross with Tom this time?
- What might happen to him?

Word level: *words from the past* **(10 mins)**

Explain to the children that in Elizabethan times a *'jumble'* was a biscuit and that Queen Elizabeth I was very fond of them.

Ask the children to collect words and phrases from Scenes 1–3 that show the play is set during the reign of Queen Elizabeth I. Where appropriate ask the children if they can think of a modern equivalent. For example: *seven of the clock, minced dates, serving men, stable lad, pastry cook, lie-a-bed.*

Independent Group Task

Word level: *identify words from the past* **(20 mins)**

Collect from Scenes 4–5 words and phrases that show the play is set in the past.

Lesson 2

Teaching Objective

- *to prepare, read and perform playscripts; compare organization of scripts with stories (T5)*

Whole Class Shared Reading

Text level: *play characteristics* **(30 mins)**

Turn to *Big Book* page 10 which contains a list of rules for setting out a playscript. Read the rules to the class and ask them to try to find an example of each rule from *A Jumble for the Queen.*

This play does not have stage directions, but explain that many plays do and these set the scene and tell the characters where to move to, how to move and how to say their lines.

Turn to *Big Book* page 11 which shows the opening of Scene 1. Ask the children to suggest appropriate stage directions. They should think how the characters might say their lines. For example *'Percival: (hot and bothered) Too fine! I'm sweating already.'*

Write their suggestions on to the acetate sheet on the lines provided.

Independent Group Task

Text level: *stage directions* **(20 mins)**

Insert stage directions using PCM 1.

Lesson 3

Teaching Objectives

- *to prepare, read and perform playscripts; compare organization of scripts with stories (T5)*
- *to practise using commas to mark grammatical boundaries (S5)*

Whole Class Shared Writing

Text level: *turning playscript into a narrative* **(15 mins)**

Look again at Scene 2 . Ask the class to help you to rewrite the scene as a narrative as if it was a chapter in a story. Ask the children how they would open the chapter. For example: *It was 7.15 in the morning as Tom hurried into school. He was late. The Master was waiting for him. 'Where have you been, Thomas?' asked the master sternly.*

Guide the children into suggesting reported speech and narrative and not just dialogue.

Sentence level: *commas to mark grammatical boundaries* **(15 mins)**

Ask the children to look again at Scene 2 and to find all the commas. Can they see any pattern in the use of commas? (They occur before the person addressed.) Explain that the comma marks off the content of the sentence from the person being spoken to.
Write on the board: *What time is it Miss?* and ask the children what punctuation is needed.

Independent Group Task

Sentence level: *commas* **(20 mins)**

Rewrite the sentences putting in the commas using PCM 2.

Lesson 4

Teaching Objectives

- *to prepare, read and perform playscripts; compare organization of scripts with stories (T5)*
- *to write playscripts, eg using known stories as basis (T13)*

Whole Class Shared Writing

Text level: *narrative to playscript* **(30 mins)**

Turn to *Big Book* page 12 and explain that this is the next scene in the play but that it is written in narrative form. Read the passage to the class and get them to answer the following questions based on this passage and their previous knowledge of the play.

- Where has the Queen travelled from and where is she going to?
- Who is the young boy?
- Why was is he running away from school?

Now turn to *Big Book* page 13 which is a play frame for the same passage. Ask the class to help you to rewrite the narrative in play form. Remind the children to add stage directions.

Independent Group Task

Text level: *writing a playscript* **(20 mins)**

Write a playscript for the following scene (Scene 7) in which Tom arrives at the kitchen where his sister Joan works, using PCM 3a or 3b as appropriate.

Lesson 5

Teaching Objectives

- *to chart the build-up of a play scene (T6)*
- *collecting and classifying examples of adverbs (S4)*
- *to spell regular verb endings (W7)*

Whole Class Shared Reading

Text level: *charting the build-up of a play* **(20 mins)**

Reread Scenes 2 and 5. What has happened in the school between these scenes? List on the board all the things that Tom has done wrong. How can we tell the Master is getting angrier? What do you think Tom will do?

Talk to the children about how Scene 2 ends at a dramatic point. Ask the children the following questions:

- Why do you think the writer then switches to a description of the Queen?
- How does this increase the tension?
- Does the same thing happen at the end of Scene 5?
- Can they think of similar techniques in TV or film?

Sentence level: *adverbs describing speech* **(10 mins)**

Look again at Scene 5. Tell the children to help you to think of adverbs which describe how each character speaks. These could be thought of as stage directions. For example, Master (*sternly*), Thomas (*meekly*), Master (*sarcastically*).

Independent Group Task

Word level: *regular verb endings* **(20 mins)**

Tell the children to look through the play and identify all the regular verbs by listing all those that end in *-s*, *-ed*, *-ing*.

Name ______________________________

Literacy World

Stage Directions

Insert stage directions in the spaces provided. The words below might be useful.

angrily crossly sheepishly nervously furiously anxiously
loudly sadly quietly sarcastically softly grinning frowning

Scene 2

Narrator Seven fifteen of the clock, and Joan's brother Tom is late for school.

Master (__________) And where is your cap, Thomas?

Tom (__________) It ...it blew away, Sir!

Master (__________) I could beat you for being late, Thomas, and I could beat you for losing your cap. Do you want to be beaten?

Tom (__________) No, Sir.

Master (__________) What is that on your satchel, Thomas?

Tom (__________) Nothing, Sir.

Master (__________) Yes it is, it's your cap, and it's wet. Why is it wet, Thomas?

Tom (__________) I .... I was catching frogs in it on the way to school, Sir.

Master (__________) I think perhaps you do want to be beaten after all, Thomas.

Teaching objective: *Y4 T1 T5 to compare organization of playscripts with stories*
Links with **Unit 3 Lesson 2**

Name ______________________

Commas

Rewrite the sentences putting in the commas.

1 Where is your homework Daniel?

____

2 Put the frog back into the pond Jane.

____

3 Amy can you go and fetch the register?

____

4 Here is your crown Your Highness.

____

5 Officer can you tell me the time?

____

6 Is this your dog Mr Jones?

____

Teaching objective: *Y4 T1 S5 to practise using commas to mark grammatical boundaries*
Links with **Unit 3 Lesson 3**

Name ______________________

Playscript Frame

You are going to write a new scene for* A Jumble for the Queen. *This scene will take place after Tom has run away and met the Queen in her coach. How do you think the scene might go? What would Tom say to his sister, Joan? What might she say to him?

Scene 7

In the kitchen of Sir Richard Ash's house. Joan is busy preparing for the Queen's visit. There is a knock at the door. It is Tom who has run away from his school.

Tom Hello, Joan! I bet you're surprised to see me. I have ______________

____

Joan (*crossly*) ______________________________________

____

Tom But the master ______________________________

Guess what? I met ______________________________

____

Joan (*turning away*) I don't believe you. You ______________

____

Teaching objective: *Y4 T1 T13 to write playscripts, eg using known stories as basis*

Links with **Unit 3 Lesson 4**

Name ____________________

Literacy World

Playscript Frame

You are going to write a new scene for* A Jumble for the Queen*. This scene will take place after Tom has run away and met the Queen in her coach. How do you think the scene might go? What would Tom say to his sister, Joan? What might she say to him?

Scene 7

In the kitchen of Sir Richard Ash's house. Joan is busy preparing for the Queen's visit. There is a knock at the door. It is Tom who has run away from his school.

Tom (*looking anxious and out of breath*) ____________________

____

Joan ____________________

____

Tom ____________________

____

Joan ____________________

____

Narrator ____________________

____

Teaching objective: *Y4 T1 T13 to write playscripts, eg using known stories as basis*
Links with **Unit 3 Lesson 4**

Unit 4

The Stove Haunting

Range: historical novel

Learning Outcomes:

Text level: investigating how settings and characters are built up from small details; to use different ways of planning stories – diagrams; to write character sketches; to explore narrative order

Sentence level: revise work on verbs; practise using commas to mark grammatical boundaries

Word level: recognizing and spelling suffixes *-ship, -hood, -ment, -ness; alphabetical order*

Lesson 1

Teaching Objective

- *to investigate how settings and characters are built up from small details (T1)*

Whole Class Shared Reading

Text level: *response to text* **(15 mins)**

Read the excerpt to the class. Ask the following questions:

- Who were the visitors to the cottage?
- How many people lived in the cottage?
- What was the matter with the baby?
- Why do you think the children didn't speak to Daniel and George?
- Why is George so angry at the end?

Text level: *how settings are built up* **(15 mins)**

Ask the children to help you to list all the things they know about the outside of the cottage (*walls – dirt or clay, holes, thatched roof, two small windows stuffed with sacking*). Ask the class to look through the rest of the story pointing out evidence of poverty.

List the suggestions on the board. Explain how the author has built up a picture of the setting through these details.

Independent Group Task

Text level: *observing details of setting* **(20 mins)**

Label the drawing of the inside of the cottage using PCM 1.

Lesson 2

Teaching Objectives

- *finding evidence of historical setting*
- *to revise work on verbs and to investigate verb tenses (S2)*
- *to investigate how settings are built up from small details (T1)*

Whole Class Shared Reading and Writing

Text level: *collecting evidence* **(15 mins)**

Reread the excerpt to the class. Ask the children to collect evidence from the text that shows that this story is not contemporary, eg *candles, iron pot, use of sacks, stone picking* etc.

- Why do you think the man is relieved when George refuses a drink?
- Why did the girl look sullen and beaten?
- How can we tell George feels sorry for the family?

Text level: *writing a setting* **(15 mins)**

Look at the opening paragraph which describes the run-down cottage. Tell the children you are going to use this as a model but they are going to describe an opposite kind of house – a grand mansion owned by a wealthy squire. Remind the children their description should be set in the last century.

Write on the board *At the end of the drive was a …*

Independent Group Task

Sentence level: *verbs* **(20 mins)**

Change the verbs into the present tense using PCM 2a or 2b as appropriate.

Lesson 3

Teaching Objectives

- *to write a character sketch, focusing on small details to evoke sympathy or dislike (T11)*
- *to recognize and spell the suffixes* -ship, -hood, -ness, -ment *(W9)*

Whole Class Shared Writing

Text level: *character sketch* **(20 mins)**

Tell the children they are going to write a character sketch of George. Explain to them he is a poor labourer in his mid-twenties. He is angry at the injustice of the society in which he lives, and he is determined to try to persuade the rich land owners to give the workers a fairer deal.

Turn to *Big Book* page 14 which lists George's actions in the story. Ask the class to decide what each of these tell us about George's character and fill in the *Big Book* page accordingly.

Word level: *suffixes* **(10 mins)**

Turn to *Big Book* page 15 which has a list of suffixes across the top. Ask the children to add suffixes to each of the words. Finally, ask them to link the definitions of the harder words to the words they define.

Independent Group Task

Text level: *character sketch* **(20 mins)**

Write up the character sketch of George started in the lesson. Use proper sentences and new paragraphs for new ideas.

Lesson 4

Teaching Objectives

- *to use different ways of planning stories – diagram (T9)*
- *to explore narrative order, identify and map out main stages of story – introductions, build-ups, climaxes, resolutions (T4)*

Whole Class Shared Writing

Text level: *planning a story* **(30 mins)**

Turn to *Big Book* page 16 which shows a story diagram with some of the details completed. Remind the children about the terms: introduction, build-up, climax and resolution. Then ask them to consider how the story might progress. Write their suggestions for the story into the box. Ask for a title.

Independent Group Task

Text level: *writing a story climax* **(20 mins)**

Write the climax from the story plan in more detail.

Lesson 5

Teaching Objectives

- *to investigate how settings are built up from small details (T1)*
- *to practise using commas to mark grammatical boundaries (S5)*
- *to use third- and fourth-place letters to sequence words in alphabetical order (W12)*

Whole Class Shared Reading

Text level: *details of setting* **(20 mins)**

Turn to *Big Book* page 17 and read out the passage from *The Stove Haunting*. This excerpt describes Daniel in the big house of the Reverend Forster, the wealthy family for whom Daniel is the kitchen boy. This passage makes an interesting contrast with the one in the *Anthology*.

Read the passage to the class and ask the following questions:

- What clues are there that this is set back in history? (*platters*)
- What evidence is there that the family is wealthy?
- What details sum up the Forsters' world?
- What details sum up Daniel's world?
- On which side of the green baize door would you rather be?

Sentence work: *commas* **(10 mins)**

Look at the use of commas in the passage. Ask the children to find examples of commas used to divide items in a list (circle these in blue) and examples of commas used to mark the grammatical boundaries within sentences (circle these in red).

Independent Group Task

Word level: *alphabetical order* **(20 mins)**

Put the words in alphabetical order using PCM 3.

Name ______________________________

Literacy World

The Cottage

This is a picture of the cottage in* The Stove Haunting *story. Reread the description of the cottage and then label all the things shown in this picture of it.

Teaching objective: *Y4 T1 T1 to investigate how settings are built up from small details*

Links with **Unit 4 Lesson 1**

Name ______________________

Literacy World

Verb Tenses

Put the verbs into the present tense.

1 Daniel and George walked to the cottage. ____________

2 George knocked on the door. ____________

3 The man asked them to come in. ____________

4 The man pointed at the loaf of bread. ____________

5 A woman rocked her baby. ____________

6 The three boys shared the single bed. ____________

7 The oldest boy nodded at Daniel. ____________

8 The other children looked at Daniel and George. ____________

9 Mr Winton refused to give them the milk. ____________

Teaching objective: *Y4 T1 S2 to revise work on verbs and to investigate verb tenses*
Links with **Unit 4 Lesson 2**

Name ______________________

Literacy World

Verb Tenses

Put the following verbs into the present tense:

1 At the end of the path was a tiny house. __________

2 There were holes in the thatch. __________

3 The crying went on and on. __________

4 George shook his head. __________

5 The bench stood by the table. __________

6 A woman sat on a pile of sacks. __________

7 They did not bother to rock the baby. __________

8 The mother shrank back on the sacks. __________

9 The baby coughed as if his chest would break in two. __________

10 She made the flour from grains of wheat. __________

Teaching objective: *Y4 T1 S2 to revise work on verbs and to investigate verb tenses*
Links with **Unit 4 Lesson 2**

Name ______________________________

Alphabetical Order

Put the words into alphabetical order:

expand	dream	drank	cried
crime	crisp	drip	explain
expert	drop	dragon	example

cried
____
____
____
____
____
____
____
____
____
____
____
____

Unit 5

Family Photo Album and *My Grandpa*

Range: poems based on a common theme

Learning Outcomes:

Text level: to compare and contrast poems on a common theme, discussing personal response; to write poems based on personal or imagined experience

Word level: to explore word rhyming; spelling by analogy

Lesson 1

Teaching Objectives

- *compare and contrast poems on similar themes discussing personal response (T7)*
- *to use independent spelling strategies – spelling by analogy (W3)*

Whole Class Shared Reading

Text level: *response to poem* **(20 mins)**

Read *Family Photo Album* to the class. Ask the following questions:

- Which is Dad's favourite photo? Why?
- Which photos feature Jake?
- Which photos feature Mum and Dad?
- How does Dad tease Mum?
- How does Mum tease Dad?
- How does Mum tease Jake?
- Why don't they take photos any more?
- Who likes having a comfort sheet?
- Did any of you have a comfort sheet or a favourite toy?
- Which verse do you think is the funniest?
- Do you like having your photo taken?
- What can we learn about the family from the poem?

Word level: *rhyme* **(10 mins)**

Ask the children to tell you the rhyming words in each verse. Write these on the board. Note which words have similar letter patterns, eg *wall/all*, and which words don't, eg *ago/know*. Do you think all the verses rhyme at the end of the second and fourth verses?

Independent Group Task

Word level: *rhyme* **(20 mins)**

Take the following words from the poem and create as many additional rhyming words as you can: *three, test, wall, leg, met, ago.* (They may not all have similar letter patterns.)

Lesson 2

Teaching Objective

- *to write poems based on personal or imagined experience (T14)*

Whole Class Shared Reading and Writing

Text level: *response to poem* **(15 mins)**

Read aloud *My Baby Sister* from *Big Book* page 18. This is another poem about family photos. Ask the children the following questions:

- Who are 'they'?
- How old do you think the child holding the baby is?
- How does the older child feel when they say *'Be careful...very very precious'.*
- There are two meanings in the last verse. What are they?
- Have you held a baby brother or sister for a photograph? How did you feel about it?
- Do you think the older child is happy to have a little sister?

Text level: *brainstorm ideas for poem* **(15 mins)**

Ask the children to recall or imagine holding a baby brother or sister. Brainstorm ideas and phrases and write these on the board.

- Think of how to describe what the baby felt like.
- Think of how to describe what the baby looked like.
- Where was the photo taken?
- How did you feel about holding your baby brother or sister?

Independent Group Task

Text level: *writing a poem* **(20 mins)**

Write a poem about a real or imagined occasion of holding a baby brother or sister using PCM 1.

Lesson 3

Teaching Objective

- *to write poems on personal or imagined experience linked to the poems read (T14)*

Whole Class Shared Reading and Writing

Text level: *response to poem* **(15 mins)**

Read *My Grandpa* to the class. Ask the children what the poet means by the following:

- *round-shouldered as a question mark*
- *led about all day by his walking stick*
- Why does the poet describe his face as a crinkled paper bag?
- What fun things does Grandpa do?
- What does the poet like best of all about his grandpa?

Text level: *writing similes* **(15 mins)**

Turn to *Big Book* page 19 which is an outline for children to create similes, as a first step in writing a poem. Ask the class to suggest similes and write these on the acetate sheet.

Independent Group Task

Text level: *writing similes* **(20 mins)**

Make up similes for a poem called 'My Gran' using PCM 2.

Lesson 4

Teaching Objectives

- *poem recall and response*
- *compare and contrast poems on similar themes (T7)*

Whole Class Shared Reading

Text level: *responding to and comparing poems* **(30 mins)**

Turn to *Big Book* page 20 and read *My Gran* to the class. Ask the following questions:

- What memories did Gran recall in the first verse?
- What do you think a tin bath was?
- What do you think the coupons were?
- Have you ever eaten rabbit stew or partridge pie?
- What were double cinema seats?
- What would you like to go back to try?

Discuss with the children what they like doing now and what they will want to tell their grandchildren about in years to come!

Ask the children which poem they preferred (*My Grandpa* or *My Gran*). Ask them what things both poems had in common (old people, fun, telling stories) and where they were different (one poem describes his grandfather's appearance, one tells you about what Gran did, one is split into verses, one has only one verse, one is rhyming, one is not).

Independent Group Task

Text level: *writing about the future* **(20 mins)**

Ask the children to write a list or a poem about what they think it will be like in sixty years' time. What do they think will have changed in the world? They might like to start '*In sixty years' time when I am 68 …*'

Lesson 5

Teaching Objective

- *to write poems based on personal or imagined experiences, linking to poems read (T14)*

Whole Class Shared Writing

Text level: *brainstorming words for a poem* **(30 mins)**

Turn to *Big Book* page 21 which contains a prompt sheet for a poem called *Old People*. Ask the children to brainstorm words and expressions to describe old people. Write their suggestions on the acetate sheet. Using the suggestions, ask them to help you to write a poem about an old person, drawing on the vocabulary they have brainstormed. Encourage them to picture the old person and also to include something of the old person's feelings and the children's attitude to him or her.

Independent Group Task

Text level: *writing a poem* **(20 mins)**

Write a description about old age using PCM 3a, or about a younger sibling using PCM 3b.

Name ______________________________

Holding the Baby

Write a poem about a real or imagined occasion of holding a baby brother or sister. Use some of the words and phrases thought up by the rest of the class earlier.

Title ____________________________________

____

____

____

____

____

____

____

____

____

____

____

____

by ________________________

Teaching objective: *Y4 T1 T14 to write poems based on personal or imagined experience*

Links with **Unit 5 Lesson 2**

Name ______________________

Gran Poem

Think of similes to go in the gaps below and create your own poem.

My Gran

My Gran is as ____________ as ______________________________

Her hair is like ______________________________

Her eyes are like ______________________________

Her face is like ______________________________

When she walks she is like ______________________________

When she sits she is like ______________________________

When she laughs she is like ______________________________

When she sleeps she is like ______________________________

The best thing about my Gran is ______________________________

____

____

Name ______________________

Poem About Old Age

Think of similes to go in the gaps below and create your own poem.

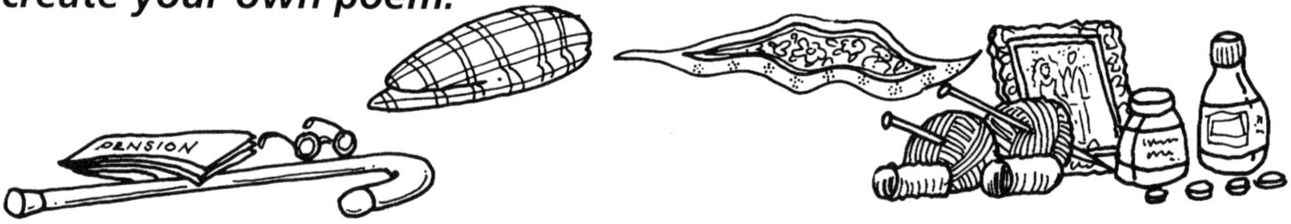

Old Folks

What do they look like?

Their hands ______________________

Their faces ______________________

Their eyes ______________________

Their clothes ______________________

How do they move?

When they walk ______________________

What are they thinking?

____

What are you thinking about them?

____

Teaching objective: *Y4 T1 T14 to write poems based on personal or imagined experience*

Links with **Unit 5 Lesson 5**

Name ______________________________

Literacy World

Brother or Sister Poem

Think of similes to go in the gaps below about a younger brother or sister and create your own poem.

My ________________________________

____________ looks like ______________________________

____________ hands are like ___________________________

____________ face is like ______________________________

____________ eyes are like _____________________________

____________ clothes are _____________________________

____________ moves like ______________________________

____________ walks like ______________________________

____________ runs like _______________________________

____________ thinks _________________________________

____

I think ____

____

Unit 6

Something Told the Wild Geese and *Snow Spell*

Range: poems based on the common theme of winter

Learning Outcomes:

Text level: to compare and contrast poems on a similar theme, discussing personal response; writing poems; brainstorming

Sentence level: revising verbs and adjectives; identifying powerful verbs

Lesson 1

Teaching Objective

- *response to poem*

Whole Class Shared Reading

Text level: *language of the poem* **(15 mins)**

Read *Something Told the Wild Geese* to the class and ask the following questions.

- What do you think told the wild geese it was time for them to go?
- Why did it not seem time for them to go?
- Why did the geese need to leave?
- Why are the fields golden?
- What do you think *lustre-glossed* means? (very shiny ripe berries)
- What do you think *amber spice* means (scent of ripe apples)
- Why are the orchards sagging?
- What do you think the last two lines mean?
- What is the rhyme scheme of the poem? (ABCBDEFE)

Text level: *form of the poem* **(15 mins)**

Reread the poem to the class paying particular attention to the metre of each line. Tell the children you are going to read the first, third, fifth and seventh lines and they are to read the intervening lines. Repeat this and then ask the children to do it with their books closed.

Independent Group Task

Text level: *rhyme scheme* **(20 mins)**

Write out the poem and underline the rhyming words, using different colours to link the rhymes.

Lesson 2

Teaching Objective

- *compare and contrast poems on a similar theme, particularly their form and language (T7)*
- *to write poems linked to poems read (T14)*

Whole Class Shared Reading

Text level: *comparing poems* **(30 mins)**

Read *Snow Spell* to the class and ask the following questions:

- What things did the family do in the place in Summer?
- What things are different in Winter?
- How do we know the river is partially frozen in the winter?
- What does it mean *the air smokes from us*?
- What are the different sounds in the Winter and the Summer?
- There are two meanings in the way the poet uses the word 'spell'. What are they?

Look at the two poems in the *Anthology*.

- Which poem is from Autumn looking to Winter?
- Which poem is from Winter looking to Summer?
- Which poem do you prefer and why?
- What aspects of nature in winter are described in the poems?

Look at the form of both poems – one has a strict rhyme scheme and one doesn't. What effect does the rhyme scheme have?

Independent Group Task

Text level: *writing a poem* **(20 mins)**

Rewrite the first verse of *Snow Spell,* describing the scene as it would have been in summer, using PCM 1.

Lesson 3

Teaching Objectives

- *to write poems, experimenting with powerful and expressive verbs (T14)*
- *identify use of poweful verbs (S3)*

Whole Class Shared Reading

Text level: *response to poem* **(20 mins)**

Turn to *Big Book* pages 22–23 which contains *Sir Winter*. Cover the last word in each verse of the poem with a 'Post-it' note. Read the poem to the class and ask them to supply the missing word. Remind them that the poem must rhyme. When they have suggested rhyming words peel off the 'Post-its' to see if their suggestions match the poet's choice.

Ask them the following questions:

- What did Sir Winter do when he first got out of bed?
- How long had he spent in bed?
- What will he do to people's houses?
- What will he do to the trees?
- How will he harden every puddle?
- How does he travel from pole to pole?
- What present does Sir Winter give to everyone in the middle of winter?

Text level: *powerful and expressive verbs* **(10 mins)**

Ask the children to find the verbs in each verse. Ask them if they help them to picture Sir Winter and what he is going to do? Explain that they are powerful and expressive verbs. Can they think of equally effective verbs that might fit in the sentences?

Independent Group Task

Text level: *reordering a poem* **(20 mins)**

Reorder the lines of the poem in the correct way using PCM 2a. Reorder the words in the lines of the poem using PCM 2b.

Lesson 4

Teaching Objective

- *using different ways of planning a poem – brainstorming (T9)*
- *to write poems based on personal experience (T14)*

Whole Class Shared Writing

Text level: *brainstorming ideas* **(15 mins)**

Ask the children to brainstorm winter words and phrases. Ask them to think about what they see, how they feel, what clothes they wear, what the animals and birds do in winter. Write their suggestions on the board.

Text level: *writing an acrostic poem* **(15 mins)**

Divide the board into two columns. Write the word '*winter*' vertically down the left-hand side of the board. Head one column '*What you see*' and the other '*What you feel*'. Ask the class to help you to write an acrostic poem about winter using some of the words and phrases they suggested earlier. *Eg,*

What you see	*What you feel*
White snow on the ground.	*Wind beating on my face.*
I	*I*
N	*N*

Independent Group Task

Text level: *writing an acrostic poem* **(20 mins)**

Ask the children to write their own acrostic poem based on summer.

Lesson 5

Teaching Objectives

- *to revise work on verbs (S2)*
- *to compare and contrast poems on particular themes, discussing personal responses and preferences (T7)*

Whole Class Shared Reading

Sentence level: *brainstorming verbs and adjectives* **(15 mins)**

Turn to *Big Book* page 24 and ask the class to think of two adjectives and one verb that could describe each of these winter words. Write their suggestions on the acetate sheet. Talk about the more effective words that the children suggest. Which words create a strong picture in their minds? Which words seem ordinary?

Text level: *discussing personal references* **(15 mins)**

Ask the class to look back at the two poems in the anthology and show them *Sir Winter* on *Big Book* pages 22–23.

Ask the children which poem they like best. They should justify their preferences by referring to lines in the text, eg *I like it when it said 'Something whispered snow.'*

Ask them to find a favourite line in each poem and explain why they chose it. Lastly, ask them if they know any other winter poems.

Independent Group Task

Text level: *evaluating poetry* **(20 mins)**

Evaluate the poetry you've read using PCM 3.

Name ______________________

Summer Poetry Frame

***This poetry frame is based on* Snow Spell.**
Write a poem about summer instead of winter.

This is our summer place

And the trees are ______________________

and all the leaves are ______________________

and the river ______________________

is ______________________

The air is ______________________

our voices ______________________

and everything is ______________________

by ______________________

Teaching objective: *Y4 T1 T14 to write poems based on personal or imagined experience, linked to poems read*

Links with **Unit 6 Lesson 2**

Name ______________________________

Poetry Jumble

Rewrite the poem on a piece of paper putting the lines within the verses into the correct order.

Sir Winter

I heard Sir Winter coming.
'I'll soon be up!' he said.
He crept out of his bed
and rubbed his thin and freezing hands:

and strew them on the floor;
'I'll shudder at the keyhole
I'll strip the trees of all their leaves
and rattle at the door,

I'll lay a sparkling quilt of snow
that Autumn thinks is his –
on everything that is!
'I'll harden every puddle

as large as any coal,
'I'll bring a load of darkness
the world, from pole to pole.
and drive my husky dogs across

'Oho! How you will shiver!'
I'll give you CHRISTMAS DAY!'
And then I heard him say:
'But in the middle of it all

by Jean Kenward

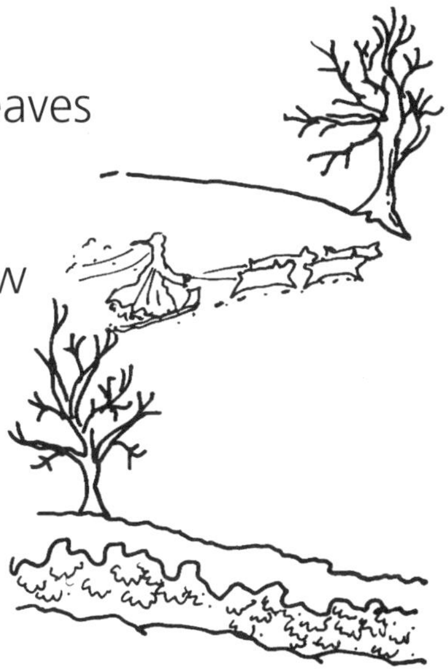

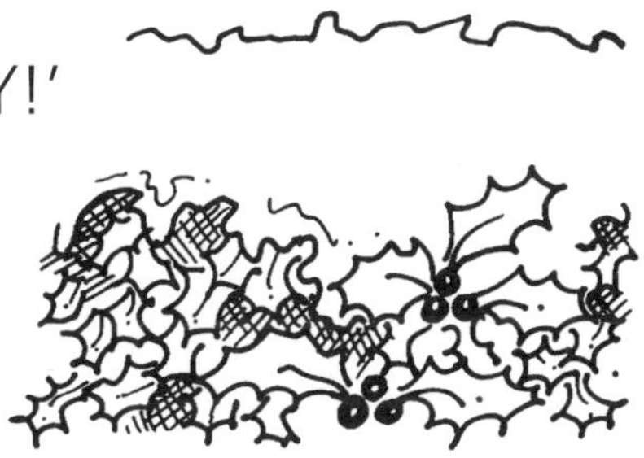

Teaching objective: *sequencing poetry*
Links with **Unit 6 Lesson 3**

Name___________________________

Poetry Jumble

Rewrite the poem putting the words in each line in the correct order. Then add punctuation.

Sir Winter

coming heard Sir I Winter
bed crept He out his of
freezing thin hands and rubbed and his
said he I'll up! be soon

keyhole I'll shudder the at
rattle and the door at
leaves their all of trees the strip I'll
them strew the on floor and

every harden puddle I'll
his is thinks that Autumn
snow I'll of lay quilt a sparkling
is! on everything that

darkness of load I'll bring a
coal as any large as
and husky drive my across dogs
the pole to world pole from

Oho! shiver! How you will
say And I heard then him
middle But the it all in of
I'll DAY! CHRISTMAS give you

by Jean Kenward

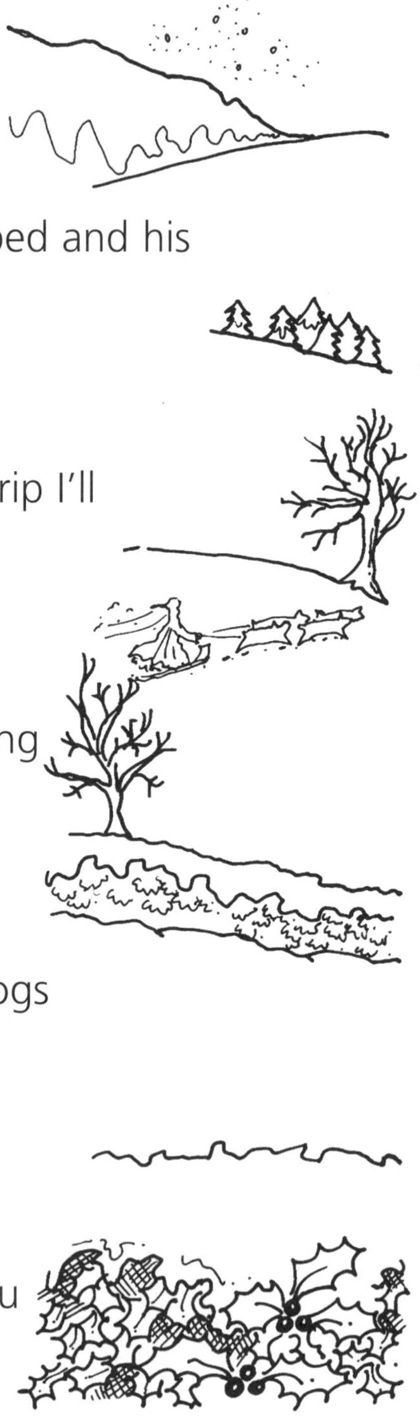

Teaching objective: *sequencing poetry*
Links with **Unit 6 Lesson 3**

Name ______________________

My Poetry Review

Winter poems

My favourite poem is ______________________

Written by ______________________

It is about ______________________

____

I like it because ______________________

____

The best line in the poem is ______________________

____

The best words in the poem are ______________________

____

Year 4 • Term 2: Literature Overview

Introduction

The range of texts for this term encompasses stories or novels about imagined worlds: science fiction; fantasy adventure; and classic and modern poetry from different cultures and times. The term begins with two stories: the first is an exciting and extremely readable piece of science fiction, and the second is a humorous fantasy story about a robot teacher. Two well-known classic poems provide a contrast to the two stories, and these are followed by the opening chapter of **The Iron Man** written by the Poet Laureate, Ted Hughes. Two modern poems complete the poetry range. Finally the children will read an extract from the final chapters of **The Hobbit** by J R R Tolkien. The texts for this term have been carefully graded so that the class will gradually become accustomed to working with more difficult prose and poetry over the weeks.

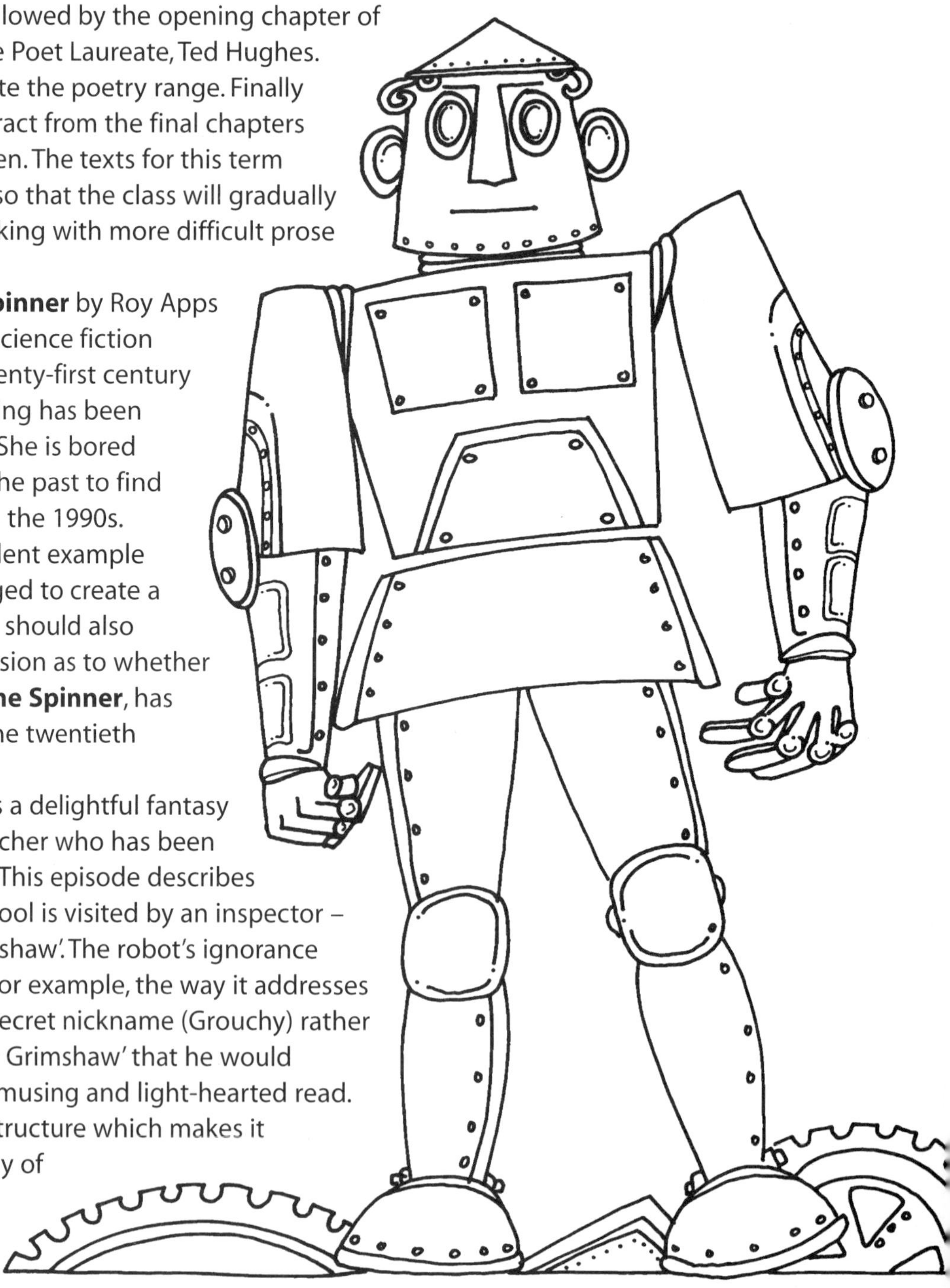

The excerpt from **Time Spinner** by Roy Apps is the opening chapter of a science fiction story. Rosemary lives in a twenty-first century space colony where everything has been programmed and sterilized. She is bored stiff and wants to return to the past to find out what it was like to live in the 1990s. This short extract is an excellent example of how an author has managed to create a believable futuristic world. It should also provoke considerable discussion as to whether or not life, as depicted in **Time Spinner**, has improved since the end of the twentieth century.

Metalmiss by Linda Pitt is a delightful fantasy adventure about a robot teacher who has been employed to teach Class 3R. This episode describes what happens when the school is visited by an inspector – the notorious 'Grouchy Grimshaw'. The robot's ignorance about certain conventions -for example, the way it addresses the school inspector by his secret nickname (Grouchy) rather than the more respectful 'Mr Grimshaw' that he would expect – makes this a very amusing and light-hearted read. The text has a clear, logical structure which makes it especially useful for the study of story development and the way that the setting can influence events.

The classic poetry unit contains **The Tide Rises, The Tide Falls** by Henry Longfellow, and **Windy Nights** by Robert Louis Stevenson. The *Big Book* contains an extract from **The Pied Piper of Hamelin** by Robert Browning and **The Eagle** by Alfred Lord Tennyson. All are well-known, classic poems which children are likely to encounter again in the future. They all have a formal, rhythmic, rhyming pattern and the punctuation is consistent throughout (for instance, a capital letter at the start of each line). They can be used to demonstrate how poetry was more fixed in form during the last century, and how the structure and choice of language identifies the poem as belonging to a previous era.

The opening of **The Iron Man** by Ted Hughes has been selected because of its powerful evocation of a believable fantasy figure. The setting of a seaside landscape heightens its authenticity. Ted Hughes makes extensive use of similes to create a vivid picture of his Iron Man. This technique can be analysed to show the children how the author has used highly expressive language as a tool to build up imagery.

The modern poetry unit consists of two mysterious poems by Jack Prelutsky and a gentle, prayer-like poem by the African poet, Lari Williams. **The Invisible Beast** and **The Troll** (the *Big Book*) describe fantasy creatures who are unknown and therefore possibly threatening. The slightly 'spooky' atmosphere of the poems is created by the arousal of expectations and a gradual build-up of tension. Children love to read something a little 'scary' when they know it's not for real, and these two poems will be greatly enjoyed by the class. In complete contrast is the poem **Before the Hunt**, with its quiet mood of prayer and contemplation.

The final unit in this term is an excerpt from **The Hobbit** by J R R Tolkien. In this passage, the dragon, Smaug, attacks the town and all seems lost. Then Bard bravely fires his last arrow towards the vulnerable hollow in the dragon's left breast, and Smaug crashes to the ground. This is a difficult piece of prose, and will need the guidance of a teacher to help the children understand the way the language has been used descriptively to create a highly imaginative scene.

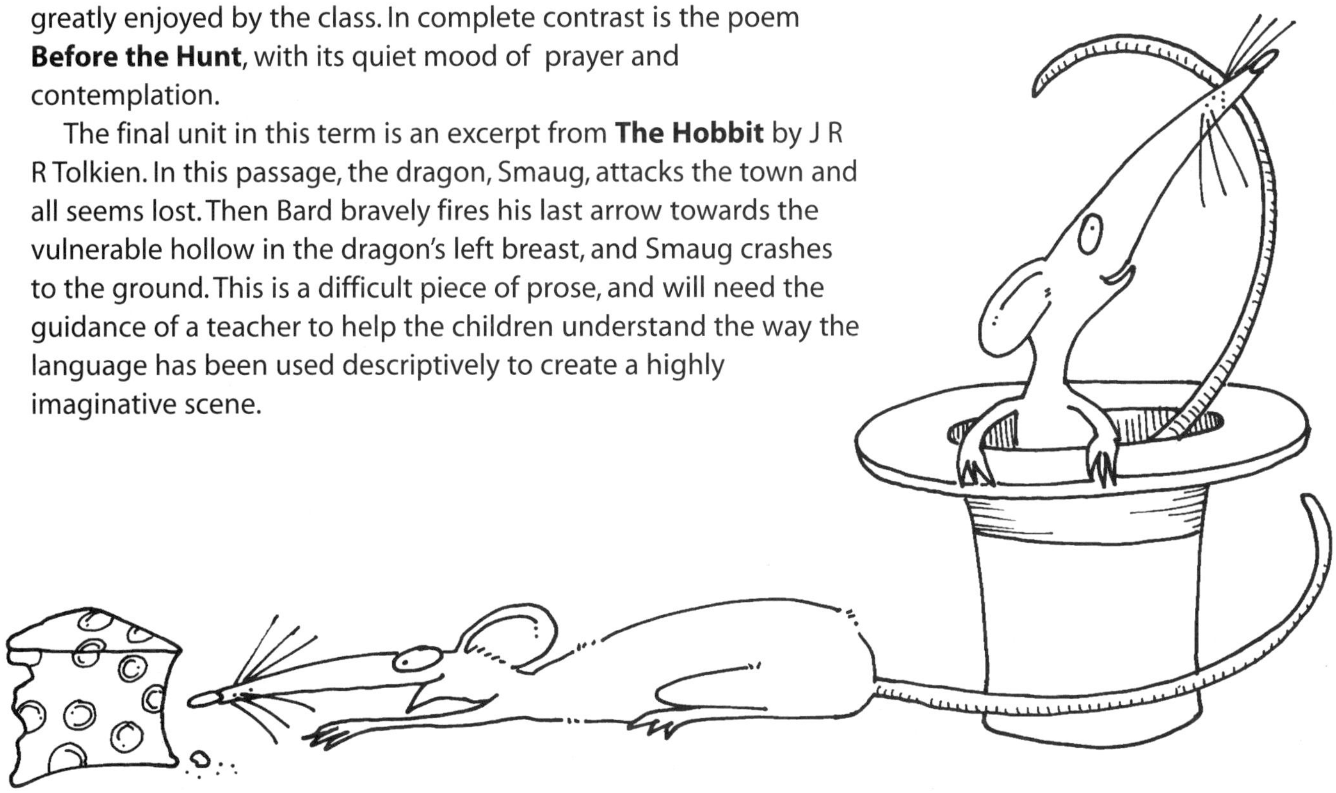

Unit 1

Time Spinner

Range: stories about imagined worlds

Learning Outcomes:

Text level: appreciation of how imaginary worlds are evoked through detail; to compare and contrast settings; to recognize how texts are targeted at particular readers; to write stories in chapters

Sentence level: to revise work on adjectives and to understand adjectives of comparison

Word level: to define familiar words; to be aware of how language changes over time; spelling of words ending in *f*

Lesson 1

Teaching Objectives

- *to understand how writers create imaginary worlds (T1)*
- *to define familiar words but within varying constraints (W12)*

Whole Class Shared Reading

Text level: *building up imaginary worlds* **(20 mins)**

Read the excerpt from *Time Spinner* to the class and ask the following questions:

- What do you think *fishes' fingers* might be? (Rosemary believes that fishes' fingers were an Elizabethan delicacy, but later finds out they were called fish fingers!)
- When do you first realize the world Rosemary lives in is different to our own? (*BedCube*)
- What does Rosemary mean when she says *'Elizabethan times'*?
- What do you think a *SupaDisk SoftWare Party* is?
- What sort of homework does Rosemary have to do?
- What things does Rosemary say *'Yawn. Bore'* about? Would you find these things boring too?
- What things are boring in your life? Would Rosemary think they were boring?
- Think about the title of the novel, and guess what Rosemary might do later on.

Word level: *define familiar words* **(10 mins)**

Ask the class how they would define the meaning of fish fingers to Rosemary. Write their suggestions on the board. Then ask the children to take out all the words which aren't absolutely essential to the definition or replace several words with one that conveys more.

Eg *Fish fingers–food–made of chopped white fish–coated with breadcrumbs–shaped like a four-sided rectangle–about 3 cm in width and 7 cm in length–nice with chips–crispy–served hot–normally grilled.*

This could be reduced to:
small oblongs of chopped fish coated in breadcrumbs.

Independent Group Task

Word level: *define familiar words* **(20 mins)**

Define familiar words using PCM 1.

Lesson 2

Teaching Objectives

- *to understand how writers create imaginary worlds (T1)*
- *to compare and contrast settings across a range of stories; to evaluate, form and justify preferences (T3)*
- *to add suffixes to words ending in* f *(W5)*

Whole Class Shared Reading

Text level: *creating settings* **(20 mins)**

Reread the extract and ask the class to list all the examples of text that hint the story is not set in contemporary times (*BedCube, number 4023,* etc). Make a list on the board and head this list *Unfamiliar to us*. Then ask the children to look through the story and find examples of things that are familiar to us (*riding a bike, arguing with parents,* etc). Write these things on the board and label the list *Familiar to us*.

Ask the children what they think of the world the author has created? Do they believe in it. Do they agree that life might be like this in the future?

Word level: *pluralization of* f *endings* **(10 mins)**

Explain that in the plural form some nouns ending in the letter *f* change the *f* to *v* before adding *es*. Write on the board: *leaf, hoof, loaf, thief, calf, half,* and then write the plural form of each. Point out that some common words break this rule (eg *chiefs, roofs*). Rub the words off the board and ask the children to write the plurals on the board.

Independent Group Task

Text level: *imagining the future* **(20 mins)**

Create your own vision of the future – what would your school, house, food, clothes be like and what would you do in your spare time?

Lesson 3

Teaching Objectives

- *to recognize how certain types of texts are targeted at particular readers; to identify intended audience (T9)*
- *to understand that vocabulary changes over time (W11)*

Whole Class Shared Reading

Text level: *identifying intended audience* **(20 mins)**

Explain to the class that they are going to consider what sort of audience certain books are intended for.

Ask the class to look at *Time Spinner* and think about how the answers to the following questions point to a particular audience:

- Through who's eyes do we see the story?
- How old would you say Rosemary is?
- What sort of things does she imagine she would like doing in the future? Are these things of interest to you?
- How realistic does her relationship with her parents seem?
- What is the effect of using words like '*Yawn. Bore*'?

Word level: *language changes over time* **(10 mins)**

Ask the children to pick out from the passage those words or phrases which sound as though they come from the future: *BedCube, DigiTuneDisk* etc.

Read out the following words from the past and ask the children what has replaced them: *wireless, frock, bathing-suit, long-player, hit parade, charabanc, counterpane.*

Independent Group Task

Text level: *language changes over time* **(20 mins)**

Identify the target audiences of various texts using PCM 2.

Lesson 4

Teaching Objective

- *to revise and extend work on adjectives – examining comparative and superlative adjectives (S1)*

Whole Class Shared Reading

Word level: *adjectives of comparison* **(30 mins)**

Remind the class that adjectives are words that describe nouns. Turn to *Big Book* pages 2–3 and explain how adjectives are normally changed into their comparative forms by adding *-er* and their superlative forms by adding *-est*. Talk through the spelling rules and fill in the blanks. Go through the rules for changing adjectives which don't conform to the normal rule and fill in the blanks.

Independent Group Task

Sentence level: *adjectives of comparison* **(20 mins)**

Consolidate understanding of adjectives of comparison with PCM 3a or 3b as appropriate.

Lesson 5

Teaching Objective

- *to collaborate with others to write stories in chapters, using plans with particular audiences in mind (T12)*

Whole Class Shared Writing

Text level: *planning chapters* **(30 mins)**

Explain that the extract from *Time Spinner* is the first chapter in the book. Ask the class why books are divided into chapters. (They structure the story, indicate new scenes, or a new event, make the story easier to read, often end on a cliffhanger so the reader will want to go on, etc.)

Tell the class that they are going to make up and map out their own story using the first chapter from *Time Spinner* as their introduction. They will need to think of a build-up, conflict and resolution and they will need to map out the events over five chapters remembering to use the chapters to best effect. Tell the children that the story should be aimed at children of their own age. Turn to *Big Book* page 4 to use the story planner.

Independent Group Task

Text level: *writing a chapter* **(20 mins)**

Choose one of the chapters from your story outline and write it in detail, remembering to use chapters to best effect.

Name ______________________

Visitors from Another Time

Imagine Rosemary has travelled back in time to the 1990s and you have to define these familiar words for her. Try to use no more than the number of words stated in brackets.

football (*10 words*)

____

____

personal stereo (*8 words*)

____

____

skateboard (*6 words*)

____

spaghetti (*4 words*)

____

trainers (*2 words*)

____

Name ______________________________

Literacy World

Who's It For?

Read these back cover blurbs and write down who you think the books are intended for and why.

Jade Zeros In
Jade and Gemma have been best friends since they left primary school and nothing's going to split them up. That is until gorgeous Brandon turns up at the school disco and suddenly there's tension in the air...

Audience: ______________________________

____

____

____

Little Sally Squirrel
Little Sally Squirrel has been collecting nuts all day and now she's tired out. But naughty Rosie Rabbit won't let her go to sleep!

Audience: ______________________________

____

____

____

Scouts in Space!
Aliens have invaded earth and there's only one person who can save the nation. It's Ernie Tuppence, leader of the 2nd Badgetown Scout Movement. Can the scout troop foil the aliens' evil plans?

Audience: ______________________________

____

____

____

Teaching objective: *Y4 T2 T9 to recognize how certain types of texts are targeted at particular readers; to identify audience*

Links with **Unit 1 Lesson 3**

Name ______________________________

Literacy World

Adjectives of Comparison

Complete the sentences with the correct comparative or superlative form of the adjective.

(small)

Rosemary's BedCube is ___small___ but her gran's is ___smaller.___

(old)

Dad has an __________ DigiTunedisc but he swapped it for an __________ one.

(large)

The __________ unit on Taurus IV is the control unit.

(dull)

Elementary Astrology is __________ but Technology is even __________.

(long)

It took a __________ time to get from Taurus to Pisces but it takes even __________ to get to Aquarius.

(big)

Our Domestic Living Unit is __________. The Williams' unit is __________ but the commanders' unit is the __________.

(fast)

Cycling is __________ but skateboarding is even __________.

(happy)

Rosemary was __________ to see Gran but even __________ to hear about Elizabethan times.

Teaching objective: *Y4 T2 S1 to revise work on adjectives, examining comparative and superlative adjectives*

Links with **Unit 1 Lesson 4**

Name ____________________________

Literacy World

Adjectives of Comparison

Complete the sentences with the correct comparative or superlative form of the adjective.

(small)
Rosemary's BedCube is __small__ but her gran's is __smaller.__

(long)
It took a _________ time to get from Taurus to Pisces but it takes even _________ to get to Aquarius.

(big)
Our Domestic Living Unit is _________. The Williams' unit is _________ but the commanders' unit is the _________.

(happy)
Rosemary was _________ to see Gran but even _________ to hear about Elizabethan times.

(hot)
All the planets are _________ but the _________ is Aquarius.

(boring)
Life on Taurus IV is _________ but school is even _____________.

(bad)
Astronomy is _________ but technology is _________.

(good)
Watching the TeleSatScreen is _________ but listening to gran's stories is _________.

Unit 2

Metalmiss

Range: stories about imagined worlds

Learning Outcomes:

Text level: how settings influence stories; expressive and descriptive language; note-making; writing settings; comparing and evaluating settings

Sentence level: using commas, connectives and full stops; possessive apostrophe

Word level: choosing more interesting words

Lesson 1

Teaching Objective

- *to understand how settings influence events and incidents in stories and how they affect characters' behaviour (T2)*

Whole Class Shared Reading

Text level: *how settings influence events and characters* **(30 mins)**

Before letting the children open the anthology tell them that they are going to read an extract about a robot. Ask them where they think the story will be set. Will it be in a fantasy world or the real world? Then tell them it is about a robot teacher in a normal school.

Ask them what sort of things might happen to a robot in a school setting. Read the extract and discuss how close their predictions were. Ask the following questions:

- Why does Metalmiss think Mr Grimshaw has come into the class?
- What are Mr Grimshaw's reasons for being in the classroom?
- What mistake does Metalmiss make when she calls Mr Grimshaw 'Grouchy'?
- Why doesn't Metalmiss understand what an inspector is?
- How does Metalmiss discover what Mr Grimshaw intends to put in his report?
- Why does Mr Grimshaw change his mind?

Ask the children to consider how Metalmiss might use her powers as a policewoman or as the prime minister. Would she be as successful as a life-saver at a swimming pool or as a footballer?

Independent Group Task

Text level: *characters in different settings* **(20 mins)**

Ask the class to write ten things that might happen if either a football team had an alien player *or* a robot is set to work on a farm.

Lesson 2

Teaching Objectives

- *to understand how the use of expressive and descriptive language can, eg create moods, arouse expectation, build tension, describe attitudes or emotions (T4)*
- *to use alternative words and expressions which are more accurate or interesting than the common choices (W9)*

Whole Class Shared Reading

Text level: *expressive language* **(20 mins)**

Turn to *Big Book* page 5 and read out the first three lines from the *Metalmiss* passage. Ask the children how Mr Grimshaw is feeling at this point. Which words tell us (*turned pale, shrank, gasped)?*

Mention how Mr Grimshaw's fear makes us expect that someone or something frightening is going to be introduced. Read the rest of the passage and ask the following questions:

- How does Mr Jones feel? Which words tell us? (*stuttered, helplessly*)
- How does Mr Grimshaw feel towards Mr Jones?
- Which words tell us? (*glared*).
- Who is not frightened or confused in this scene?
- How do we know that Metalmiss is in control? (*cold stare, swivelled* and clear speech)

Read the next *Big Book* page, which is the same passage with all the descriptive words taken out, and discuss the effect.

Word level: *more interesting words* **(10 mins)**

Using *Big Book* page 6, ask the children to suggest more interesting words for the words in red. Ask them to add adjectives and adverbs where possible and try to make them different from the words used in the original.

Independent Group Task

Word level: *more interesting words* **(20 mins)**

Rewrite the passage using more interesting words on PCM 1.

Lesson 3

Teaching Objectives

- *note-making: to edit down a sentence or passage by deleting the less important elements (T14)*
- *to use the apostrophe accurately to mark possession (S2)*

Whole Class Shared Reading and Writing

Text level: *note-making* **(15 mins)**

Tell the class that they are going to help you write an edited down version of what happens to Mr Grimshaw up to line 24. Reread this part of the story. Discuss which events are important and which are not important. Write them down on the board and ask the class to help you order them. The notes should come to less than 40 words.

Sentence level: *apostrophes* **(15 mins)**

Turn to *Big Book* page 7, read the sentences and explain how the apostrophe tells the reader to whom the object belongs. Ask the children to fill in the blanks. Then explain that when the owner is plural the apostrophe goes after the final *s*. Ask the children to fill in the blanks. Continue practising apostrophes on *Big Book* page 8.

Independent Group Task

Sentence level: *apostrophes* **(20 mins)**

Consolidate use of the apostrophe with PCM 2a or 2b.

Lesson 4

Teaching Objectives

- *to develop use of settings in own writing (T10)*
- *to recognize how commas, connectives and full stops are used to join and separate clauses (S4)*

Whole Class Shared Writing

Text level: *creating settings* **(20 mins)**

Tell the class that they are going to go on a fantasy adventure to an imagined land and that they are going to describe that land in detail. Decide whether the class will travel to another time on earth or whether they will go to another planet altogether. What will this place look like? What sort of plants and creatures will there be? Will it be friendly or dangerous? Start the piece of writing off on the board with '*The spaceship door slid open and one by one we entered the new world...*' Encourage the use of adjectives and expressive language.

Sentence level: *commas, connectives and full stops* **(10 mins)**

Read out the piece of writing on the board and review the use of commas, connectives and full stops. Briefly recap how these are used and ask the children to suggest where others might be added or swapped around to improve this piece of writing.

Independent Group Task

Text level: *note-making* **(20 mins)**

Ask the class to look again at *Metalmiss* from line 83 to the end, and ask them to write notes on what happens in this passage. They should write their notes in not more than 80 words.

Lesson 5

Teaching Objective

- *to compare and contrast settings across a range of stories; to evaluate, form and justify preferences (T3)*

Whole Class Shared Reading

Text level: *comparing and evaluating stories* **(30 mins)**

Recap what happened in *Time Spinner* in the previous unit. Ask the class what the similarities were between *Time Spinner* and *Metalmiss* (*both about children the same age, both have humour, both have element of fantasy*).

Ask what the main differences were. Bring out particularly that *Metalmiss* is about a fantasy creature in a real setting and *Time Spinner* is about a real girl in a fantasy setting. Ask the class which story they preferred and ask them to justify their preferences. Talk more generally about books they have read and whether they prefer fantasy settings or real-world ones.

Independent Group Task

Text level: *writing extension of story* **(20 mins)**

Fill in Mr Grimshaw's report on Pinkerton Primary School using PCM 3.

Name ______________________

Interesting Words

Rewrite this passage swapping the words in bold for more interesting ones. Look at the box of words below if you need help.

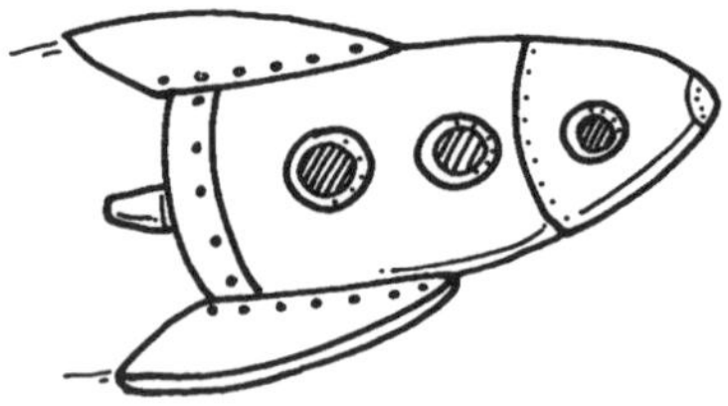

Zak was feeling **bad** but he managed to **go** to his spacecraft, open the door and **get** himself in. Then he **got** open his bag and **felt** deep within it. 'Where have I put my activation key?' he **said**. In the distance he heard the **scary noise** of the aliens' missiles moving steadily closer. **Then** Zak's **shaking** fingers felt something **metal** and he **got** out the key.

Then the spacecraft **shook** into life, and with a **loud noise** it **went** up into the sky.

finally	soared	terrible	terrifying	haul	roar	suddenly
rummaged	muttered	wailing	trembling	metallic		
whipped	juddered	tore	stagger			

____

____

____

____

____

____

____

Teaching objective: *Y4 T2 W9 to use alternative words which are more interesting than the common choices*

Links with **Unit 2 Lesson 2**

Name ______________________

Literacy World

Adding the Apostrophe

Add the apostrophe to show ownership.

The boys watch *The boy's watch*

The boys watches *The boys' watches*

The girls book ______________________

The girls books ______________________

The dogs collar ______________________

The dogs collars ______________________

The ships anchors ______________________

The ships anchor ______________________

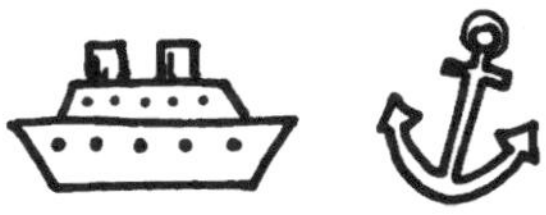

The horses saddles ______________________

The horses saddle ______________________

The boys cloakroom ______________________

The boys cloakroom ______________________

Teaching objective: *Y4 T2 S2 to use the apostrophe accurately to mark possession*
Links with **Unit 2 Lesson 3**

Name ______________________

Adding the Apostrophe

Add the apostrophe to show ownership.
Decide whether the owner is singular or plural.

The cats tail *The cat's tail*

The cats tails *The cats' tails*

The mens boots ______________

The mans boots ______________

The ladys bag ______________

The ladies bags ______________

The lions mane ______________

The lions manes ______________

The childrens clothes ______________

The childs clothes ______________

The womans gloves ______________

The womens gloves ______________

The animals foot ______________

The animals feet ______________

Teaching objective: *Y4 T2 S2 to use the apostrophe accurately to mark possession*
Links with **Unit 2 Lesson 3**

Name ______________________________

Literacy World

Inspector's Report

School: *Pinkerton Primary School*

Inspector: *Mr Grimshaw*

First impressions of school:

Good points

- ______________________________
- ______________________________
- ______________________________

Weak Points

- ______________________________
- ______________________________
- ______________________________

Best lesson observed:

I went into 3R's science lesson and ______________________________

____

____

Best teacher:

- ______________________________

Final comments:

- ______________________________
- ______________________________

signed ______________________________

Mr Grimshaw *(School Inspector)*

Teaching objective: *Writing extension of story*

Links with **Unit 2 Lesson 5**

Unit 3

The Tide Rises, the Tide Falls and *Windy Nights*

Range: classic poems

Learning Outcomes:

Text level: to identify clues which suggest poems are older; to identify different patterns of rhyme and verse; to understand the use of figurative language in poems; to write poetry based on the structure and/or style of poems read

Sentence level: to understand significance of word order

Word level: to understand how vocabulary changes over time

Lesson 1

Teaching Objectives

- *to identify clues which suggest that poems are older (T6)*
- *to understand how language changes over time (W11)*

Whole Class Shared Reading

Text level: *understanding the poem* **(20 mins)**

Read the poem to the class. Explain some of the less familiar vocabulary, eg *tide, curlew, hastens, efface, steeds, ostler.*

Read the poem again and ask the children to join in the last line of each verse.

Ask the following questions:

- What time of day is it in each verse?
- Who is hurrying towards the town?
- Why are the waves described as having *soft white hands*?
- What happens to the footprints?
- What do the horses do when the ostler calls them?
- Why do you think the traveller doesn't return?
- Why does the poet repeat '*And the tide rises, the tide falls*'?
- What different things call in each verse?
- Do you think this is a happy, sad or mysterious poem?

Text level: *archaic language* **(10 mins)**

Ask the class to identify the clues which suggest that this poem was written a long time ago.

Point out the archaic words and old-fashioned use of language (*sea-sands, the traveller hastens, steeds, ostler, but nevermore*). Write these words or phrases on the board and discuss with children the modern equivalent.

Independent Group Task

Text level: *understanding archaic language* **(20 mins)**

Write out the poem changing the archaic words into everyday language.

Lesson 2

Teaching Objective

- *to identify different patterns of rhyme and verse in poetry and read these aloud effectively (T7)*

Whole Class Shared Reading

Text level: *performing the poem* **(20 mins)**

Turn to *Big Book* page 9 which contains an excerpt from the long narrative poem *The Pied Piper of Hamelin*. Tell the story of how the Pied Piper rid the town of Hamelin of rats but when he was not paid his fee, he charmed the children out of the town and they were never seen again.

Read the poem to the class twice and then divide up the lines for choral reading as follows:

Line 1	Whole class
Line 2	One child first half and second child to end of line.
Line 3	Child 3
Line 4	Child 4
Line 5	Child 5
line 6	Child 6
Line 7	All boys
Line 8	All girls
Line 9	$\frac{1}{3}$ of class
Line 10	$\frac{2}{3}$ of class
Line 11	Whole class

Practise this until the performance is fluent.

Text level: *rhyme pattern* **(10 mins)**

Underline the words that help the children to work out the rhyme scheme (AABABAAACCA).

Independent Group Task

Text level: *identify rhyme patterns* **(20 mins)**

Replace the missing rhyming words using PCM 1.

Lesson 3

Teaching Objectives

- *to understand the use of figurative language in poetry (T5)*
- *to identify different patterns of rhyme and verse in poetry, and to read these aloud effectively (T7)*
- *to understand the significance of word order (S3)*

Whole Class Shared Reading

Text level: *understanding the poem* **(20 mins)**

Read *Windy Nights* to the class and ask the following questions:

- What does the *stars are set* mean?
- When does the rider gallop about?
- What does *the trees are crying aloud* mean?
- Who do you think the rider is?
- Why might he be galloping about on windy nights?
- Is the poem happy, sad or mysterious?
- Which words are repeated? Why?
- As you listen to the poem what rhythm do you think the poet is trying to capture?
- What clues are there that this poem is not a poem describing life today? (mention of fires, man riding horse)

Now ask the children to read it with you trying to capture the sense of galloping hooves. Ask half the class to tap out the sound of the hooves while the others say the lines softly and mysteriously.

Sentence level: *word order* **(10 mins)**

Write the following sentences on the board:
Only children eat bacon crisps. (ie not adults)
Children only eat bacon crisps. (ie they don't do anything else with bacon crisps)
Children eat only bacon crisps. (ie they don't eat any other flavours)
Children eat bacon crisps only. (ie they don't eat anything else at all)
Point out how the meaning changes on the position of *only*.

Independent Group Task

Text level: *word order* **(20 mins)**

Change the order of words using PCM 2.

Lesson 4

Teaching Objectives

- *to understand the use of figurative language in poetry (T5)*
- *to identify different patterns of rhyme and verse in poetry (T7)*

Whole Class Shared Reading

Text level: *understanding the poem* **(30 mins)**

Turn to *Big Book* page 10 and read *The Eagle* to the class. Ask the following questions:

- What do they think the poet means when he says: *He clasps the crag with crooked hands*?
- In what ways is the eagle close to the sun?
- Why does the poet mention *lonely lands*?
- What do you think *Ring'd with the azure world* means?
- In what ways does the eagle fall like a thunderbolt?
- What is the poet making us think of when he describes the claws of the eagle as *crooked hands*?
- Why do you think the sea is described as *wrinkled*?
- Why does he say the sea *crawls* beneath the eagle?
- What effect does the alliteration have on the poem?
- Work out the rhyme scheme. (AAA BBB)

Brainstorm words to describe the eagle (*powerful, majestic, cruel, solitary, observant*).

Independent Group Task

Text level: *identifying rhyme patterns* **(20 mins)**

Fill in the missing words of the poem using PCM 3a, or put the words in the right order using PCM 3b.

Lesson 5

Teaching Objective

- *to write poetry based on the structure and/or style of poems read (T11)*

Whole Class Shared Writing

Text level: *writing a poem* **(30 mins)**

Ask the children what features all the poems have in common (each line begins with a capital letter; rhyming pattern; regular rhythm or metre; they all use less familiar language).

Ask the class to jointly construct a poem which has some of these features. Base the poem on the rhyme scheme of *The Eagle* and remind children that the last word in the first line should have many rhyming possibilities. Try to maintain the stressed beat of each line. The children could choose another bird as the subject of each line of the poem.

Independent Group Task

Text level: *learning a poem* **(20 mins)**

Working with a partner learn by heart *Windy Nights*.

Name ______________________

Literacy World

Rhyming Poem

Put the rhyming words in the box below back into the poem:

cats	ladles	vats	speaking	hats
cradles	chats	squeaking	flats	sprats

Rats!

They fought the dogs and killed the ______________

And bit the babies in the ______________

And ate the cheese out of the ______________

And licked the soup from the cooks' own ______________

Split open the kegs of salted ______________

Made nests inside men's Sunday ______________

And even spoiled the women's ______________

By drowning their ______________

With shrieking and ______________

In fifty different sharps and ______________

Teaching objective: *Y4 T2 T7 to identify different patterns of rhyme and verse in poetry*
Links with **Unit 3 Lesson 2**

Name ______________________

Word Order

Make as many different sentences as you can using the words in the box. You can use each word over and over again.

most	some	our	school	team	teachers	girls
boys	football	games	food	in	on	the
Wednesday	Monday	like	play			

1 *Some girls like football on Monday.*

2 ______________________

3 ______________________

4 ______________________

5 ______________________

6 ______________________

7 ______________________

8 ______________________

9 ______________________

10 ______________________

Teaching objective: *Y4 T2 S3 to understand significance of word order*
Links with **Unit 3 Lesson 3**

Name ___________________________

Fill in the Gaps

Fill in the gaps with the words from the box. To help you, note that the rhyme pattern is AAA/BBB.

hands	sun	world	crag	lands	stands
falls	sea	mountain	thunderbolt	walls	crawls

The Eagle

He clasps the __________ with crooked __________;
Close to the __________, in lonely __________,
Ring'd with the azure __________, he __________

The wrinkled __________ beneath him __________;
He watches from his __________ __________,
And like a __________ he __________.

by Alfred, Lord Tennyson

Teaching objective: *Y4 T2 T7 to identify different patterns of rhyme and verse in poetry*
Links with **Unit 3 Lesson 4**

Name ______________________________

Poetry Jumble

Write out the poem putting the words in each line in order.
To help you, note that the rhyme pattern is AAA/BBB.

The Eagle

He with crooked clasps the hands crag
lands in to Close sun the lonely
he world, with azure Ring'd the stands

wrinkled The crawls sea beneath him
walls watches from He his mountain
falls And thunderbolt like he a

by Alfred, Lord Tennyson

The Eagle

____

____

____

____

____

____

by Alfred, Lord Tennyson

Teaching objective: *Y4 T2 T7 to identify different patterns of rhyme and verse in poetry*
Links with **Unit 3 Lesson 4**

Unit 4

The Iron Man

Range: novel about imagined world

Learning Outcomes:

Text level: the use of figurative language, especially similes; to understand how writers create imaginary worlds; the use of expressive, descriptive language

Sentence level: to revise and extend work on adjectives

Word level: using alternative words; to explore how suffixes can be added to nouns to make adjectives; spelling words with common endings

Lesson 1

Teaching Objectives

- *story recall and response*
- *revise and extend work on adjectives (S1)*

Whole Class Shared Reading

Text level: *response to story* **(20 mins)**

Read the opening of the story to the class and ask the following questions:

- Where do you think the Iron Man might have come from?
- How do we know the size of the Iron Man?
- What happened when he stepped off the cliff?
- What two parts of the Iron Man did the gulls pick up?
- What did the gulls think the eye was?
- What did they think the hand was?
- What happened when the hand and the eye got together?
- What part of his body could the Iron Man not find?
- What does the Iron Man do at the end of the excerpt?
- Where is the story set?
- Why do you think the rocky beach is a good setting for how the Iron Man rebuilds himself?

Sentence level: *adjectives* **(10 mins)**

Ask the children to look again at lines 1–32 and to collect all the occasions when the adjective '*iron*' is used, eg *iron fingers, great iron head, iron ears.* Ask the children why they think the author has chosen to repeat this word. What effect does this have in helping us to visualize the Iron Man?

Independent Group Task

Sentence level: *adjectives* **(20 mins)**

Look back through the excerpt and collect all the words that create the setting of the story, eg *high cliff, rocky beach, sea, seagulls.*

Lesson 2

Teaching Objective

- *to understand the use of figurative language, locate use of simile (T5)*

Whole Class Shared Reading and Writing

Text level: *similes* **(30 mins)**

Reread the story to the class. Remind the children what similes are – that they liken one thing to another. Then look at *Big Book* page 11 which contains three of the similes from the story. Ask the children what two things are being compared in each case and the effect of the comparison. Ask the children to find examples of other similes in the excerpt, eg line 40 and line 71. Then ask the children to help you to construct new similes to describe the Iron Man. Write these suggestions in the appropriate place on the acetate sheet.

Independent Group Task

Text level: *creating similes* **(20 mins)**

Create similes to describe the Iron Man using PCM 1.

Lesson 3

Teaching Objectives

- *to attend to the detail of the story*
- *revision of work on verbs*
- *to use alternative words and expressions (W9)*
- *to understand how writers create imaginary worlds (T1)*

Whole Class Shared Reading

Text level: *attending to detail* **(30 mins)**

Ask the children to listen very carefully as you reread from line 72 to line 112 of *The Iron Man.* This describes how the Iron Man rebuilds himself. Help the children to visualize each stage of the rebuilding process by using their hands to replicate the actions being described, eg the hand stood up on three fingers.

Then look at *Big Book* page 12. This passage from the story has some of the verbs deleted. Ask the children to suggest suitable verbs to fill the gaps. Write these on the acetate sheet. List other optional verbs on the board. Discuss other words which are more interesting or accurate. Finally, ask the children to look in their anthologies and to compare their choice of verbs with the verbs the author has used.

Independent Group Task

Text level: *sequencing* **(20 mins)**

Sequence the section of the story where the Iron Man rebuilds himself, using PCM 2.

Lesson 4

Teaching Objective

- *adding suffixes to nouns to make adjectives (W13)*

Whole Class Shared Reading

Word level: *suffixes* **(30 mins)**

Turn to *Big Book* page 13 which shows examples of words used first as nouns and then transformed into adjectives by adding different suffixes. Remind the children about nouns (naming words) and adjectives (describing words). Point out how the spelling of the noun sometimes changes when the suffix is added. Work through the examples, explaining the role each word is playing in the phrases.

Independent Group Task

Word level: *suffixes* **(20 mins)**

Add suffixes to nouns to make adjectives, using PCM 3a or 3b as appropriate.

Lesson 5

Teaching Objectives

- *to write own examples of descriptive, expressive language based on those read (T13)*
- *to spell words with common endings (W6)*

Whole Class Shared Reading and Writing

Text level: *awareness of expressive language* **(10 mins)**

Tell the children that, in some ways, the story is written more like a poem than prose. Find examples of this from the text, eg one-word sentences; one-line paragraphs; onomatopoeic words; repetition of description; powerful verbs; use of similes and metaphors.

Ask the children to speculate why the author has chosen to do this.

Text level: *using expressive language* **(20 mins)**

Point out to the children that we are told in great detail what the Iron Man looks like and what he does but the author does not tell us what the Iron Man is thinking or what his personality is like.

Tell the children that they are going to imagine that they are the Iron Man and they are going to explain what he is thinking at each stage of the story. Look at *Big Book* pages 14–15. This lists different events in the story.

Ask the children to speculate about what the Iron Man might be thinking at that moment. Encourage them to think carefully about word choices as they make their suggestions. Write the best suggestions on the acetate sheet.

Independent Group Task

Word level: *words with common endings* **(20 mins)**

Ask the children to make as many words as they can using the following letter patterns: *ear, ound, ould, ost*. These can be at the end of a word or in the middle.

After ten minutes they should compare lists with a partner. They should score one mark for any word they have in common and two marks for a word only one child has written. Then ask the children to add up their scores.

Name ______________________

Literacy World

Similes

Write your own similes to describe the parts of the Iron Man labelled.

The Iron Man was like ______________________ .

Teaching objective: *Y4 T2 T5 to understand figurative language, similes*
Links with **Unit 4 Lesson 2**

Name ______________________

Sequencing

Sequence the action as the Iron Man rebuilds himself. (The first one has been done for you.)

[1] When the hand picked up the eye it began to look for other parts of the Iron Man. The seeing hand found an arm but it was stuck between two rocks.

[ ] The strange trio found the other eye. The seeing hand fitted it to the blind hand. Next they found a leg.

[ ] They found the other leg and the other arm. Now each arm, hand and eye rode on a leg.

[ ] They found the head in a heap of red seaweed. The Iron Man fitted it back in place.

[ ] The two hands tugged the arm out from the rocks, and the seeing hand fastened itself to the wrist of the arm. They made a strange trio.

[ ] The seeing hand found the other hand and led it back to the arm.

[ ] They jumped on top of the leg and guided it to look for the missing parts.

[ ] One found an ear and the other found the giant torso.

[ ] They fitted the legs and arms to the torso and went searching for the head.

Teaching objective: *Sequencing*
Links with **Unit 4 Lesson 3**

Name ____________________________

Nouns to Adjectives

Add the suffix* -ful *to make these nouns into adjectives:

telling the truth ____truthful____

full of hope ________________

in a lot of pain ________________

achieves success ________________

offering help ________________

got some uses ________________

Add the suffix* -y *to make these nouns into adjectives:

lots of rocks ________________

full of water ________________

a bad smell ________________

full of dirt ________________

lots of rain ________________

lots of dust ________________

Teaching objective: *Y4 T2 W13 suffixes that can be added to nouns to make adjectives*

Links with **Unit 4 Lesson 4**

Name ______________________________

Literacy World

Nouns to Adjectives

Add the suffixes* -ful, -ic, -al, -ible, -able *to change these nouns into adjectives.

comfort	a	*comfortable*	chair
hero	an	______________	character
peace	a	______________	sleep
music	a	______________	boy
dread	a	______________	accident
success	a	______________	result
reason	a	______________	explanation
wash	a	______________	jumper
nation	the	______________	anthem
horror	a	______________	dress
angel	an	______________	smile
fashion	a	______________	style
grace	a	______________	dancer
joy	a	______________	occasion
occasion	an	______________	treat
volcano	a	______________	eruption

Teaching objective: *Y4 T2 W13 suffixes that can be added to nouns to make adjectives*
Links with **Unit 4 Lesson 4**

Unit 5

The Invisible Beast and *Before the Hunt*

Range: modern poetry including poems from different cultures

Learning Outcomes:

Text level: to understand how the use of expressive and descriptive language can build tension; to understand the use of figurative language; to identify different patterns of rhyme; to write poetry based on examples of descriptive, expressive language

Sentence level: to compare adjectives on a scale of intensity

Word level: to explore implications of words which imply gender

Lesson 1

Teaching Objectives

- *to explore how expressive language can build tension (T4)*
- *to identify different patterns of rhyme and verse in poetry, eg rhyming couplets, and to read these aloud effectively (T7)*

Whole Class Shared Reading

Text level: *expressive language* **(20 mins)**

Read *The Invisible Beast* to the class. Ask the children which lines are repeated in the poem and suggest why the poet might have chosen to do this. Reread the poem and experiment with different ways of reading the repeated couplet at the end of each stanza. Is it more effective spoken in whispered tones or in a dark sinister voice?

In some ways the fear described in the poem is like a nightmare. Ask the children what gives the poem its nightmare quality (*unseen horror; unable to scream for help; helpless*). Ask which words describe the movement of the beast (*stalking; footsteps falling*); the beast itself (*frightful features; ungainly form; awful smell*). Which is more frightening – a beast that is described in detail or one that is left to your imagination?

Reread the poem with individual children reading two lines each and the whole class joining in for the repeated final two lines of each verse.

Text level: *rhythm and rhyme* **(10 mins)**

Ask the children to find the rhyming words in verse 1. What is the rhyme pattern? (ABCBDEFE) Is it the same for the other stanzas? Ask the children to listen to the metre of each line (4 stressed beats) and then to identify the rhythm of each line: '*The beast that is invisible*'. Show how the regular rhythm is maintained even though the number of words in each line varies.

Independent Group Task

Text level: *expressive writing* **(20 mins)**

Ask the children to add details to the unspecified description of the beast. They should describe its *frightful features* and *great ungainly form* and its *awful smell*. They should title their writing: *The Visible Beast*.

Lesson 2

Teaching Objectives

- *to understand the use of expressive language (T4)*
- *to understand the use of figurative language (T5)*
- *to identify different patterns of rhyme (T7)*

Whole Class Shared Reading

Text level: *rhyme* **(15 mins)**

Before showing children *Big Book* page 16 (*The Troll*), use 'post-its' to cover the following rhyming words: *hole; plate; pot; bones; legs; gulp; go; troll.* Explain to the class that the rhyme scheme is ABAB in each verse. Then read the poem and ask the children to guess what the covered words might be. Record their guesses on the board. Then reveal the poet's original words and compare the results. Read the poem again with the class joining in.

Text level: *figurative and expressive language* **(15 mins)**

Ask the children to identify the following from the poem:

- A powerful adjective to describe the troll *(loathsome)*.
- Two adjectives that describe his blood *(black, boiling hot)*.
- An example of alliteration (*gurgles, ghastly, groans*).
- Four verbs that describe what the troll will do when he catches you (*catch, clutch, grind, swallow*).
- An example of onomatopoeia (*gobble! gobble! gulp!*).
- A simile *(like scrambled eggs)*.

Independent Group Task

Text level: *creating moods* **(20 mins)**

Fill in the gaps in the poem using PCM 1.

Lesson 3

Teaching Objectives

- *to identify different patterns of rhyme and verse in poetry and to read these aloud effectively (T7)*
- *to explore and discuss the implications of words which imply gender (W10)*

Whole Class Shared Reading

Text level: *verse pattern* **(20 mins)**

Read the poem *Before the Hunt*. This Nigerian poem describes the hunter's prayer before he sets off to trap his prey. Ask the following questions:

- What words are repeated in the poem? (*me, as the*) What effect does this repetition have? (prayer-like quality).
- Which words describe the wind (*howling, chilling*); the trees (*dancing*); the breeze (*cooling*); the sky (*guiding*); the forest (*living*); the shadows (*teasing*)?
- What do all these words have in common?
- Why is the sky described as *guiding*? And the moon as *lonely*?
- Find the similes in the poem.

Divide the poem for choral reading as follows: different groups to read lines 1, 3, 5, 7, and the first half of 19, 20 and 21, interspersed with a solo voice of the hunter.

Word level: *words that imply gender* **(10 mins)**

Tell the children that certain words imply gender, eg prince/princess; king/queen. Sometimes the female form is created by adding the suffix *-ess*. Ask the children the alternative gender form for the following: *woman, emperor, steward, waiter, madam, widow, tiger, female.*

Independent Group Task

Word level: *words that imply gender* **(20 mins)**

Consolidate understanding of words that imply gender using PCM 2.

Lesson 4

Teaching Objectives

- *to write poetry based on the structure of a poem read (T11)*
- *comparing adjectives on a scale of intensity (S1)*

Whole Class Shared Writing

Text level: *writing a poem* **(20 mins)**

Using the structure of *Before the Hunt,* create a class poem in which the adjectives are substituted (*howling, dancing, cooling, guiding, living, chilling, teasing*). Explain that the children are to think of alternative verbal adjectives to replace the originals. These adjectives will always end in *-ing.* Decide upon the most appropriate and write these to make the class poem.

Sentence level: *adjectives of intensity* **(10 mins)**

Turn to *Big Book* page 17 and explain how a group of adjectives can mean roughly the same thing but at different levels of intensity. Sort the groups of adjectives into order of intensity. Then think of two more verbal adjectives escalating in intensity.

Independent Group Task

Sentence level: *adjectives* **(20 mins)**

Supply adjectives on a scale of intensity using PCM 3a or 3b as appropriate.

Lesson 5

Teaching Objective

- *to write poetry based on the structure of a poem (T11)*

Whole Class Shared Writing

Text level: *writing a poem* **(20 mins)**

Look again at the poem *The Invisible Beast*. Remind the children that the poem has an ABCBDEFE rhyme scheme. Tell the children that you are going to create a class poem with the same rhyme and rhythm. You will use some of the phrasing from the original poem, eg

The Beast that is invisible
is __________ through the park.

Ask the children to suggest alternatives for: *sense, ungainly, cosy, safe, awful, beating faster, falling, scream.*

Sentence level: *punctuation in poems* **(10 mins)**

Study the use of capital letters in the three poems. Ask the children where the capital letters are used in *The Invisible Beast*. How does this compare with *The Troll*? How are they used differently in *Before the Hunt*? Discuss why the poets have made these decisions. Look at other punctuation in *The Troll.* Find examples of: apostrophe to denote omission; use of the dash; exclamation marks.

Independent Group Task

Text level: *writing poetry* **(20 mins)**

Tell the children to write their own prayer, like *Before the Hunt,* asking for good luck in some activity, eg winning a football match.

Name ______________________

Write a Scary Poem

Fill in the gaps with powerful adjectives.

Be wary of the __________ troll		*(adjective)*
That __________ lies in wait		*(adverb)*
To drag you to his __________ hole		*(adjective)*
And put you on his plate.		
His blood is __________ and __________ hot		*(two adjectives)*
He __________ __________ groans		*(verb + adjective)*
He'll __________ you in his dinner pot		*(verb)*
Your skin, your flesh, your bones.		
He'll _______ your arms and _______ your legs		*(verbs)*
And __________ you to a pulp		*(verb)*
Then swallow you like ____________________		*(a simile)*
__________ __________ gulp!		*(onomatopoeia)*
So watch your step when next you go		
Upon a __________ stroll,		*(adjective)*
Or you might end in the __________ below		*(noun)*
As __________ for the troll.		*(noun)*

Teaching objective: *Y4 T2 T4 to understand how the use of expressive and descriptive language can create moods*

Links with **Unit 5 Lesson 2**

Name ____________________

Gender Words

Find the masculine and feminine and write them in pairs below.

husband	niece	cow	hero	brother	nephew	vixen	
heroine	king	bridegroom	uncle	lion	heir	duke	
sister	queen	wife	duchess	bull	fox	bride	aunt
lioness	heiress						

husband *wife*

Change the following sentences from masculine to feminine.

The bridegroom was an heir.

The king had a lion.

The waiter served the duke.

The fox attacked the drake.

My uncle kept a billy goat.

Teaching objective: *Y4 T2 W10 to explore and discuss the implications of words which imply gender*

Links with **Unit 5 Lesson 3**

Name________________________

Adjectives of Intensity

Put the following adjectives in order of intensity.

1	hot	boiling	lukewarm	warm
	______	______	______	______
2	ecstatic	happy	delighted	pleased
	______	______	______	______
3	huge	enormous	big	gigantic
	______	______	______	______
4	sad	miserable	upset	wretched
	______	______	______	______
5	tired	drowsy	sleepy	exhausted
	______	______	______	______
6	starving	peckish	ravenous	hungry
	______	______	______	______
7	freezing	chilly	cold	cool
	______	______	______	______

Teaching objective: *Y4 T2 S1 comparing adjectives on a scale of intensity*
Links with **Unit 5 Lesson 4**

Name ____________________

Literacy World

Adjectives of Intensity

Fill in the missing adjectives to complete the scale of intensity for each of these groups of adjectives.

lukewarm	*warm*	*hot*	boiling
pleased	____	____	ecstatic
big	____	____	gigantic
upset	____	____	wretched
drowsy	____	____	exhausted
irritated	____	____	furious
peckish	____	____	ravenous
worried	____	____	petrified
able	____	____	genius
cool	____	____	freezing

Unit 6

The Hobbit

Range: novel about imagined world – fantasy adventure

Learning Outcomes:

Text level: to understand how writers create imaginary worlds; to understand how settings influence events; notemaking – to edit down a passage

Sentence level: to revise and extend work on adjectives; apostrophe for contraction and possession; to recognize how punctuation is used to join and separate clauses

Word level: prefixes *al-, mis-*

Lesson 1

Teaching Objectives

- *activating prior knowledge*
- *story recall and response*
- *recognizing and spelling the prefixes al-, mis- (W7)*

Whole Class Shared Reading

Text level: *understanding the story* **(20 mins)**

Before reading the excerpt to the class, brainstorm any knowledge they have about dragons (eg *can fly; guard treasure; breathe fire; fight knights*). Ask the children how they have acquired this knowledge. Read the excerpt to the class.

After reading the excerpt, check what has been learned about dragons from the passage and compare this with the list of items provided by the children. Then ask the following questions:

- Were the townsfolk prepared for the dragon's attack? Find all the evidence.
- What weapons did the people use?
- What defences did Smaug have?
- How does Tolkien describe the number of arrows fired at the dragon?
- What were Smaug's plans when the people tried to escape in boats?
- Who was the captain of the archers?
- How did he discover the dragon's weak spot?
- What happened to the dragon?

Word level: *prefixes* **(10 mins)**

Write the on the board: *all ways*. Tell the children that when the prefix *al-* is added to a word it has only one *l*. Write *always* on the board. Ask the children how you should combine: *all most, all so, all though, all ready, all together*.

Write on the board: *miss take*. Explain how we write *mistake* as one word. Combine the following: *miss fit, miss fire, miss fortune, miss understand, miss print*.

Independent Group Task

Word level: *vocabulary extension* **(20 mins)**

Find an unfamiliar word in each of the paragraphs from line 47 onwards. Write the word, what you think it means in the context and then what the dictionary says. (Suitable words: *hindered, huddled; wither; yew; perched; hollow; silvered; forge; glittered.*)

Lesson 2

Teaching Objectives

- *to understand how writers create imaginary worlds (T1)*
- *to revise and extend work on adjectives (S1)*
- *to recognize how commas, connectives and full stops are used to join and separate sentences (S4)*

Whole Class Shared Reading

Text level: *description of imaginary character* **(20 mins)**

Reread the story to the class and encourage the children who checked up on new vocabulary to share their findings.

Turn to *Big Book* pages 18–19 and show the class the picture of Smaug, the dragon. Tell the children that they are going to label the picture based on descriptions in the text. Using the acetate sheet, write the descriptions of each part of the dragon. Then encourage the children to think of suitable adjectives to describe other parts of Smaug (his eyes, back, claws, etc).

Sentence level: *commas* **(10 mins)**

Explain to the class that Tolkien uses complex sentences which are divided by commas to help the reader. Look at line 13 (*Every vessel in the town…*). Read it to the class, pausing for the appropriate punctuation, then ask a child to read it.

Next, look at line 34 (*No one had dared…*). Ask children to prepare a reading of that sentence and then share their readings. Ask them to explain why they chose to pause when they did. Do the same with other complex sentences with embedded clauses.

Independent Group Task

Text level: *sequencing* **(20 mins)**

Sequence the story using PCM 1.

Lesson 3

Teaching Objectives

- *to understand how writers create imaginary worlds (T1)*
- *to understand how settings influence events (T2)*
- *notemaking – to edit down a passage (T14)*

Whole Class Shared Reading

Text level: *building a scene* **(20 mins)**

Explain to the children that you are going to explore how Tolkien creates the scene of the attack by Smaug. They are going to find evidence from the text of how the setting is built up.

Look at *Big Book* page 20 which contains details of descriptions under the headings: *Sights* and *Sounds.* Ask the children to find further examples and (using the acetate sheet) add these to list.

Text level: *notemaking* **(10 mins)**

Look at the two paragraphs beginning with lines 19 and 27. Ask the children to read the paragraphs silently and then discuss what is essential to the action and what is additional description. Ask them how to cut it down to a brief summary with only the essential material. For example: *Smaug swooped again and again, destroying the buildings. The people tried to put out the flames. They shot at Smaug but their weapons were useless.*

Independent Group Task

Text level: *writing from character's point of view* **(20 mins)**

Write Bard's account of the battle with Smaug, using PCM 2.

Lesson 4

Teaching Objective

- *distinguishing between uses of the apostrophe for contraction and possession (S2)*

Whole Class Shared Reading

Sentence level: *apostrophes* **(30 mins)**

Turn to *Big Book* page 21 which revises work on using the apostrophe to show that something belongs to someone. Then it gives examples of the apostrophe to show contraction (revision from year 3). Finally, it draws attention to the words 'its' and 'it's'.

Independent Group Task

Sentence level: *apostrophes* **(20 mins)**

Add apostrophes to show contraction and possession using PCM 3a or 3b as appropriate.

Lesson 5

Teaching Objectives

- *to understand how writers create imaginary worlds, and evoke it through detail (T1)*
- *revise and extend work on adjectives (S1)*
- *to recognize how commas, connectives and full stops are used to join and separate clauses (S4)*

Whole Class Shared Reading

Text level: *description of an imaginary creature* **(20 mins)**

Turn to *Big Book* page 22 and read the excerpt from the opening chapter of *The Hobbit*, which describes what a hobbit is like. Encourage the class to visualize the description.

Using the acetate sheet, underline all the adjectives and adjectival phrases which describe a hobbit. Ask the children what we can predict about the type of hero Bilbo Baggins will be, based on this introduction.

Sentence level: *punctuation* **(10 mins)**

Look again at *Big Book* page 22 and ask the children to find examples of the following uses of punctuation: question marks; commas; full stops; connectives. Ask the children how the punctuation helps the reader to interpret the passage.

Independent Group Task

Text level: *observing detail* **(20 mins)**

Create a 'Wanted' poster for Bilbo Baggins. Give accurate details where possible, eg name, appearance; and invent unknown information, eg age, personality.

Name ______________________________

Literacy World

Sequencing

Put the following events in the correct order. The first one is done for you.

1	With a terrible roar Smaug approached the town. He saw that the bridge was down so he swept over the town.
	The arrows made Smaug's rage grow.
	People jumped into boats to escape the burning buildings.
	Smaug was killed.
	Smaug was so angry he circled high in the air, then he swooped with fire leaping from his jaws.
	Bard, the captain of the archers, is informed by a thrush where he can find Smaug's weak spot.
	Many buildings were set alight.
	The people fired arrows at Smaug but the arrows fell back uselessly into the lake.
	Bard fired his black arrow which pierced the unprotected part of Smaug's belly.

Teaching objective: *Sequencing*
Links with **Unit 6 Lesson 2**

Name ______________________________

Literacy World

Bard's Account of the Battle with Smaug

Fill in Bard's account of the battle with Smaug using descriptive language.

I could see Smaug's plan was to burn the town. I didn't care if ________

____

I had fired all my arrows except ______________________________

Suddenly out of the dark something fluttered to my shoulder ________

____

The thrush said ____

____

I drew my bow string to my ear and spoke to my arrow ____________

____

____

As the dragon swooped I let the arrow go and ___________________

____

____

Teaching objective: *Y4 T2 T13 to write own examples of descriptive and expressive language based on those read*

PCM 2

Links with **Unit 6 Lesson 3**

Name ______________________

Apostrophes

Add apostrophes where the letters are missing and then write out the words in their full form.

isnt	______	dont	______
cant	______	hes	______
weve	______	theyve	______
couldnt	______	youve	______
shouldnt	______	wouldnt	______
Id	______	wed	______

Now add apostrophes to show who owns what.

Harjinders bag
the ladys book
the mens books
Karls chair
The ladies bags
The mans sock

Put the apostrophe in the right place in the following conversation.

'Its time for school.'
'Its not!'
'Yes it is.'
'But its only 8.00.'
'Well, its about time you were early for once!'

Now add its (as in belonging to it) to the following conversation.

The cat chases ______ tail.
______ tail is long and furry.
______ teeth nearly touch ______ tail.
One day it might bite ______ own tail.

Teaching objective: *Y4 T2 S2 to use the apostrophe accurately to mark possession through distinguishing between uses of the apostrophe for contraction and possession*

Links with **Unit 6 Lesson 4**

Name ____________________

Literacy World

Apostrophes

Add apostrophes to show where letters are missing. Then write out the words in their full form.

theyll	____________	couldnt	____________
well	____________	Id	____________
whos	____________	mustnt	____________
theyd	____________	shouldnt	____________
wont	____________	wed	____________
youll	____________	shed	____________

Now add the apostrophe to show who owns what.

my cats whiskers	childrens feet
Yasmins dog	foxs cubs
the womans gloves	boxes lids
the wolves den	babys tooth
the mouses tail	babies teeth

Decide whether this conversation uses **its** ***(as in belonging to it) or*** **it's** ***(as in it is). Put the apostrophes in the right places.***

'Has the dog had its dinner?'

'Its waiting for it.'

'Its waiting for its dinner?'

'Yes, its sitting by its food bowl with a hungry look on its face.'

Teaching objective: *Y4 T2 S2 to use the apostrophe accurately to mark possession through distinguishing between uses of the apostrophe for contraction and possession*

Links with **Unit 6 Lesson 4**

PCM 3b

Year 4 • Term 3: Literature Overview

Introduction

The range of texts for this term concentrates on stories and short novels which raise issues. This is followed by a wide selection of different types of poetry: haiku; epitaphs; alphabet; lists; and thin poems. Some of these use a simple rhyming format, whilst others are constructed in free verse. The poems have been deliberately grouped together to be studied during the last weeks of this term. Each form can be addressed in one or two Shared Reading sessions which is easier to manage when there are so many other end of term activities taking place.

Basia's Birthday Present by Robin Mellor is set in Poland. It is a very moving story about a girl who is upset because she has not received any birthday presents. Then her grandmother tells her about a new-born baby who has nothing, and whose family are worrying about another mouth to feed. Basia makes a doll from tiny scraps of material and gives it to the baby. She comes to realize that this has made her happier than any present she might have been given. This story highlights the issue of poverty in Europe, and also raises questions about our priorities and where they should lie. Finally, it will emphasize to the children that the expense of a gift is not as important as the thought that goes into it.

Anne Fine is an author whose books deal primarily with the various difficult situations and and moral dilemmas that are likely to confront children on a day-to-day basis. She very skillfully manages to take a serious situation and present it in an amusing way, without detracting from the seriousness of the topic. **The Diary of a Killer Cat** presents the cat's point of view on the death of a bird. No one likes to see a small bird killed, but at the same time the reader is encouraged to appreciate how the natural instinct of the cat has to be accepted. **Bill's New Frock** is famous for raising awareness of the different treatment that girls and boys tend to receive. This excerpt is taken from the first chapter of the book, when Bill wakes up to discover that he's turned into a girl. This is a excellent book for Shared Reading sessions, and should lead to some lively debate amongst the children. It is recommended that Anne Fine is adopted as 'author of the term', and that the children should try to make a class collection of her books and evaluate them.

Cheat! by Judy Waite is part of Literacy World's Guided Readers. It demonstrates how one small lie can lead to more and more lies, and how the only way to prevent the escalation is to face the truth before the situation gets out of hand. Danny's grandmother enters a painting in a competition, believing that it was painted by Danny. Because he badly wants his grandmother to be proud of him, Danny allows her to carry on believing the lie. However the painting wins the competition and Danny is awarded the first prize of £50. In an effort to put things right he donates the money to the Society for the Blind. Everyone then praises Danny for his generosity and he realizes that, far from salvaging the situation, he is now in even deeper water. Most children have told the odd 'fib' or 'small white lie' for one reason or another, and will therefore be able to identify with Danny's dilemma. The class should be encouraged to explore the issues raised by the author, and to appreciate that there are no easy solutions to the problems that result from telling lies.

The collection of poems by popular contemporary children's writers like Wes Magee and Tony Bradman are amusing and challenging, and will introduce the children to the terminology of many different forms (rhyme, rhythm, alliteration, stanza, verse and couplet). This is a 'fun' note on which to end the term, and should whet the appetite for poetry in many children. The poems are short and accessible, using the simplest form and language, and will provide excellent models for the children to use for their own poetry writing.

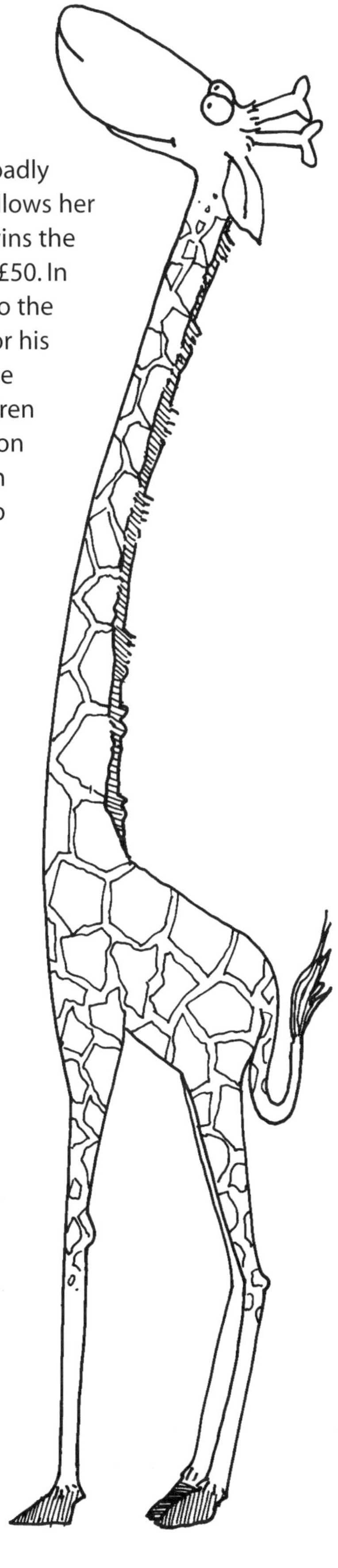

Unit 1

Basia's Birthday Present

Range: stories from other cultures

Learning Outcomes

Text level: identifying differences in stories from other cultures; identifying social, moral or cultural issues in stories; identifying the dilemmas faced by characters; writing alternative endings for a story

Sentence level: understanding how the grammar of a sentence alters when the sentence type is altered; changing words

Word level: spell words with common letter strings but different pronunciations

Lesson 1

Teaching Objectives

- *to read stories from other cultures, by focusing on differences in place, time, customs, relationships (T2)*
- *vocabulary extension*
- *to identify social, moral or cultural issues; to locate evidence in text (T1)*

Whole Class Shared Reading

Text level: *response to story* **(20 mins)**

Before reading the story to the class, ask the children to guess what Basia's birthday present might be. Collect some initial suggestions. Then explain that Basia is very poor and ask the children for alternative suggestions. Finally, tell the children that Basia is a Polish refugee. Explain what refugees are. Now what present do they think Basia might expect?

Read the story to the class and ask the following questions:

- Why is Basia crying at the beginning of the story?
- What food does Basia eat for supper and lunch?
- What does Basia decide to do for the baby?
- How does Grandmother help Basia?
- Do you think Basia minds that she does not receive any presents?
- How would you feel if you received no presents on your birthday?
- What clues are there that this story is not set in Britain?
- There are many things in the story we are not told. Guess answers to the following: where is Basia's father/grandfather? Why are they refugees? Where are they going? Are they in danger? Why?

Word level: *vocabulary extension* **(10 mins)**

Find the following words in the story:
Paragraph 1: a word to describe how the wind blew (*howled*); para 3: how the candle burned *(flickered*); para 7: an adjective to describe the soup *(watery*); para 9: the apostrophe to show omission *(wasn't);* para 10: a word to describe falling asleep *(drifted*); para 13: a word to describe a snowstorm *(blizzard*).

Independent Group Task

Text level: *finding evidence* **(20 mins)**

Collect evidence from the passage that indicates how poor Basia is, eg *'thin ragged coat', 'ruined buildings', 'no presents', 'watery soup'.*

Lesson 2

Teaching Objectives

- *reading in role*
- *to understand that words can be changed in particular ways (S1)*

Whole Class Shared Reading and Writing

Text level: *reading in role* **(15 mins)**

Reread the story as a play. You should take the part of the narrator and ask children to read the parts of Basia, her mother, her grandmother and the baby's mother.

Sentence level: *changing words* **(15 mins)**

Turn to *Big Book* page 2 which shows a sentence from the story with each word labelled according to its class. Point out how each of these words can be changed. Explain that verbs can change tense; nouns can be singular or plural and adjectives can be comparative. Then ask the class to suggest how the words listed can be changed and write in the different forms in the spaces provided.

Independent Group Task

Sentence level: *changing words* **(20 mins)**

Consolidate understanding of which words can be changed and how using PCM 1.

Lesson 3

Teaching Objectives

- *to understand how the grammar of a sentence alters (S3)*
- *to explore the main issues of a story (T11)*

Whole Class Shared Writing

Sentence level: *changing sentences* **(30 mins)**

Turn to *Big Book* page 3 about changing sentences into different forms. Work through the statements from the story, changing them first into question form and then into negative statement form. The first one has been done as an example. Point out to the class what changes are made to the words and word order as the sentences are changed.

At the bottom of the page there is a space for children to list the changes that are made when statements are changed to negatives and questions. Help the children decide upon a list of things that change, eg word order, verb tense, new words required, question mark required.

(Extra sentences: *Basia tried to sleep. Basia tied the buttons on to the doll's head. The baby was lying in his mother's arms.*)

Independent Group Task

Text level: *story dilemmas* **(20 mins)**

Complete the cloze procedure on Basia's diary using PCM 2.

Lesson 4

Teaching Objectives

- *to write critically about an issue or dilemma raised in a story, explaining the problem, alternative courses of action and evaluating the writer's solution (T8)*
- *to spell words with common letter strings but different pronunciations (W6)*

Whole Class Shared Reading and Writing

Text level: *solving character's problems* **(20 mins)**

Turn to *Big Book* page 4 and ask the children to read the 'problems' faced by Basia and to decide what the author's solutions were. Write the author's solution after the red bullet. Then ask the children to consider how they might have solved the problem. Write this suggestion after the green bullet. Finally, open out the discussion for children to decide if they agree with Grandmother that '*to give is better than to receive*'.

Word level: *common letter strings with different sounds* **(10 mins)**

Write the following words on the board: *wait, hair, said*. Ask the children what the words have in common. Point out that all three words have the same letters in the middle but those letters make different sounds in each word. Ask the children to distinguish the separate sounds in each word. Do the same with: *look, room, door*. Ask the children if they can think of other *oo* words which make the same sound as the *oo* in *look*. Then do the same with *door* and *room*.

Independent Group Task

Word level: *common letter strings with different sounds* **(20 mins)**

List words with the same letter string but different pronunciations using PCM 3a or 3b as appropriate.

Lesson 5

Teaching Objective

- *to write an alternative ending for a known story (T12)*

Whole Class Shared Writing

Text level: *writing alternative storylines* **(30 mins)**

Turn to *Big Book* page 5 which offers alternative courses of action open to Basia at the point when her grandmother tells her about the baby. Ask the children to suggest how these storylines might develop. Using the acetate sheet, write their suggestions in the spaces provided.

Independent Group Task

Text level: *writing an alternative ending* **(20 mins)**

Choose one of the alternative endings and write it as continuous prose.

Name ______________________

Changing Words

What changes can be made to these verbs?
Follow the example of run.

run	*runs*	*running*	*ran*
walk	______	______	______
swim	______	______	______
go	______	______	______
teach	______	______	______

***What changes can be made to these* adjectives?**
***(Be careful with the spelling – do you need to double the consonant or change the* y *into* i *and add* er/est?)**

cold	*colder*	*coldest*	happy	______	______
thin	______	______	hungry	______	______

***What changes can be made to these* nouns?**

hand *hands* baby ______ doll ______ blanket ______

present ______ candle ______ boot ______ eye ______

Underline any of the following words which cannot be changed:

mother when hope so and sat

new until call into birthday but

PCM 1

Teaching objective: *Y4 T3 S1 to understand that words can be changed*
Links with **Unit 1 Lesson 2**

Name ____________________

Literacy World

Basia's Diary

***Fill in the gaps to retell the story of* Basia's Birthday Present.**

I stood in the doorway. There were ____________ in my eyes. It was my ____________ but I had no ____________.

My mother told me that she couldn't ____________ to buy any presents.

I sat next to my ____________ and ate some watery ____________. Grandmother told me about a family who had just had a new ____________. That night I couldn't ____________. I felt so ____________ for the baby who had nothing for his birthday.

In the ____________ I looked for something that could be a present for the baby. When Grandmother saw what I had ____________ she said, 'Make a ____________.' So I ____________ a doll with the sacking and stuffed it with ____________. The straw was sticking out at the top. I thought it looked like ____________. But my doll did not have any ____________.

Grandmother felt around under her ____________. She pulled out two ____________. I put them on the doll and they looked like ____________ eyes.

I took it to the new baby. His mother said, 'It's ____________.'

Then I felt better and did not mind so much about ____________ having a present but I hope I get one next ____________.

Teaching objective: *Y4 T3 T11 to explore the main issues of the story*
Links with **Unit 1 Lesson 3**

Name ______________________

Common Letter Strings

The words in the boxes have the same letter strings but different pronunciations. List together all the words that sound the same.

ow

howled	blown	snowed
cow	now	know

how	yellow
howled	________
________	________
________	________

ou

would	mouth	thought	should
found	brought	ground	fought

could	sound	bought
________	________	________
________	________	________
	________	________

ea

reach	hear	thread	eat	
clear	dead	dream	year	head

each	spread	ear
________	________	________
________	________	________
________	________	________

Teaching objective: *Y4 T3 W6 to spell words with common letter strings but different sounds*

Links with **Unit 1 Lesson 4**

Name ____________________

Common Letter Strings

The words in the boxes have the same letter strings but different pronunciations. List together all the words that sound the same.

ow

howled	blown	snowed
cow	now	know

how ________ yellow ________

howled ________

________ ________

________ ________

ou

mouth	could	enough	out	found
though	would	young	bought	you

should ________ thought ________ soup ________ around ________ shoulders ________ rough ________

________ ________ ________

____

ea

greater	dead	each	eat	dream
create	thread	beauty	spread	

head ________ reach ________ great ________ beautiful ________

________ ________ ________

________ ________

Teaching objective: *Y4 T3 W6 to spell words with common letter strings but different sounds*
Links with **Unit 1 Lesson 4**

Unit 2

Diary of a Killer Cat and *Bill's New Frock*

Range: stories by the same author

Learning Outcomes

Text level: understanding how paragraphs or chapters are used to collect, order and build up ideas; identifying social, moral or cultural issues in stories; reading further stories by a favourite writer, making comparisons and identifying familiar features of the writer's work; identifying the dilemma faced by characters; exploring the main issues of a story

Sentence level: revising common punctuation marks

Word level: using the apostrophe and distinguishing its and it's; examining words with common roots

Lesson 1

Teaching Objectives

- *to identify social, moral or cultural issues in stories (T1)*
- *to understand how paragraphs or chapters are used to collect, order and build up ideas (T3)*

Whole Class Shared Reading and Writing

Text level: *response to story* **(20 mins)**

Read *Diary of a Killer Cat* to the class and ask the following questions:

- What genre of writing is this?
- How do you know?
- What do you think the next chapter will be called?
- What did Tuffy do on Monday?
- Does he feel sorry for what he did?
- What did the family do on Tuesday?
- What do you think will happen on Wednesday?
- How has the author used the chapters to order ideas and build up the events?

Text level: *finding evidence* **(10 mins)**

Tuffy has killed the bird and squashed the plants. What defence does he give for these offences? Make a list on the board of Tuffy's justifications.

Independent Group Task

Text level: *diary writing* **(20 mins)**

Ask the children to write Ellen's diary for the same Monday. Remind them to use paragraphs to order their ideas.

Lesson 2

Teaching Objectives

- *to explore humour in writing*
- *to identify the common punctuation marks (S2)*
- *distinguishing its and it's (W10)*

Whole Class Shared Reading

Text level: *exploring humour* **(20 mins)**

Reread the excerpt to the class. Much of the humour derives from the fact that we are viewing events from the cat's point of view. Ask the children to find examples of how Tuffy is describing events to gain sympathy from the reader. Turn to *Big Book* page 6 which shows two columns, one for Tuffy's point of view and the second for the family's point of view. Fill in the gaps in each column.

Sentence level: *identifying punctuation* **(10 mins)**

Ask the children to find examples of the following punctuation in *Killer Cat* and to say how it helps us to understand the passage:

- apostrophe to show omission
- apostrophe to show possession
- hyphens
- question marks
- brackets

Independent Group Task

Sentence level: *inserting punctuation* **(20 mins)**

Punctuate a section from the story using PCM 1.

Lesson 3

Teaching Objective

- *to identify social, moral or cultural issues in stories, eg the dilemmas faced by characters (T1)*

Whole Class Shared Reading

Text level: *considering an issue* **(30 mins)**

Read the excerpt from the novel *Bill's New Frock*.
Ask the following questions:

- How is life different for Bill Simpson now he is a girl? How do his parents, Mean Malcolm and the elderly lady treat him?
- Whose behaviour towards Bill has not altered?
- Do you think it is a dream or is it more like a nightmare?
- What is the dilemma facing Bill?
- How would you feel if you were treated as a member of the other sex?
- Why do you think people treat boys and girls differently?
- This is a story with a message. What do you think the message is?

Independent Group Task

Text level: *considering an issue* **(20 mins)**

Consider which activities are associated with boys and which with girls using PCM 2.

Lesson 4

Teaching Objective

- *collect/classify words with common roots (W7)*

Whole Class Shared Reading

Word level: *Latin roots* **(30 mins)**

Big Book page 7 shows some Latin words with their translations and a list of English words which derive from the Latin root. Discuss the meaning of the words and see if the children can link the meaning back to the root word. Encourage them to add words based on the root words provided. Other examples for aqua are: aquatic, Aquarius, aquarium, aquaduct.

liber:	liberty, liberal, library
centum:	century, centigrade, centipede
factum:	factor, factory, fact
audio:	audible, audience, audio-visual
signum:	signpost, signal, significant

Encourage children to be on the look out for further examples of the root word when they are reading.

Independent Group Task

Word level: *vocabulary extension* **(20 mins)**

Look back through the story and pick out any words that are less familiar. List these words and check their meaning in the dictionary. (Possible words: *fiddly, dismay, savagely, piercing, sprawled, grasped, hauling.*)

Lesson 5

Teaching Objectives

- *to read further stories by a favourite writer, identifying familiar features of the writer's work (T9)*
- *to write critically about an issue or dilemma raised in a story, explaining the problem, alternative courses of action and evaluating the writer's solution (T8)*
- *to explore the main issues of a story (T11)*

Whole Class Shared Reading and Writing

Text level: *discussing a writer* **(30 mins)**

Ask the children if they can think of other books by Anne Fine (*Goggle-eyes, Madam Doubtfire, Only a Show, Stranger Danger, How to Write Really Badly* are a few examples).

Look at *Big Book* page 8 which has information on some of Anne Fine's books. One of the recurring features of Anne Fine's writing is the humour with which she approaches characters' dilemmas and problems. Read through the issues in the stories and discuss the way Anne Fine has made the situation humorous in each case. What is the common theme?

Look at the headings for *Diary of a Killer Cat* and *Bill's New Frock* on *Big Book* page 9. Identify and write down what the issues and humour are. Encourage the children to see the similarities even though the stories are very different.

Independent Group Task

Text level: *writing a diary entry* **(20 mins)**

Complete a cloze procedure on the Wednesday diary entry for Tuffy using PCM 3a or write Tuffy's diary entry for Wednesday using PCM 3b.

Name ______________________

Literacy World

Punctuation

Write out the following passage from* Diary of a Killer Cat *putting in punctuation where it is needed.

Oh, Tuffy she says, all sniffles and red eyes and piles of wet tissues. Oh Tuffy. How could you *do* that

How could I *do* that I m a *cat*. How did I know there was going to be such a giant great fuss, with Ellies mother rushing off to fetch sheets of old newspaper, and Ellies father filling a bucket with soapy water

Okay, *okay*. So maybe I shouldnt have dragged it in and left it on the carpet. And maybe the stains wont come out, ever so *hang* me

____

____

____

____

____

____

____

Teaching objective: *Y4 T3 S2 to insert the common punctuation marks*
Links with **Unit 2 Lesson 2**

Name ______________________

Literacy World

Who Can Do What?

Some people have clear ideas about what boys should do and what girls should do. Tick whether these people would think the following activities were for boys or girls.

	Boys	Girls
Play rugby		
Enjoy reading		
Have a favourite football team		
Like skipping		
Like fashionable hair-styles		
Wear make-up		
Be kind to younger children		
Like pets		
Work hard at school		
Offer to help the teacher		
Build Lego		
Play computer games		
Play football at playtime		
Write neatly		
Like pop music		

Do you agree?

____

Do you think that some things are only for boys and some only for girls?

____

Teaching objective: *Y4 T3 T1 to identify social, moral or cultural issues in stories*
Links with **Unit 2 Lesson 3**

Name ____________________

Literacy World

Tuffy's Diary

Fill in the gaps in Tuffy's diary for Wednesday.

Wednesday

So spank me! I brought a dead mouse into their precious house. I didn't even kill it. When I came across __________, it was already a goner. Nobody's safe around __________. This avenue is ankle-deep in rat poison, fast cars charge up and __________ at all hours, and I'm not the only __________ around here. I don't even __________ what happened to the thing. All I know is, I found __________. It was __________ dead. (Fresh dead, but dead.) And at the time I thought it was a good __________ to bring it home. Don't ask me why. __________ must have been crazy.

How did I know that Ellie __________ going to grab me and give me one of her little talks?

'Oh __________! That's the second __________ this week. I can't bear it. I know you're a __________ and it's natural and everything. But, __________ for my sake, stop.'

She gazed into my __________.

'Will you __________? Please?'

I gave __________ the blink. (Well, I tried. But she __________ having any.)

'I mean it, Tuffy,' she told __________. 'I love __________, and I understand how you feel. But you have got to __________ doing this, okay?'

She had me by the paws. What __________ I say? So I tried to look sorry. And then she burst into __________ all over again and __________ had another funeral.

This place is turning __________ Fun City.

It really is.

Teaching objective: *Y4 T3 T11 to explore main issues of a story*

Links with **Unit 2 Lesson 5**

Name ____________________

Literacy World

Tuffy's Diary

Use the prompts to write Tuffy's diary for Wednesday. (Remember to write everything from Tuffy's point of view.)

Wednesday

So spank me! I bought a dead mouse into their precious home.

____

____

____

Of course when Ellie saw the mouse she ______________

____

____

____

All I did was ______________________

____

____

People have no idea what life is like for a cat!

Teaching objective: *Y4 T3 T11 to explore main issue of a story*
Links with **Unit 2 Lesson 5**

Unit 3

Cheat!

Range: stories that raise issues

Learning Outcomes

Text level: to identify social, moral or cultural issues; to explore an issue by writing a story about a dilemma; to write critically about a dilemma raised in a story; paragraphing

Sentence level: to understand how the grammar of a sentence is altered when the sentence type is altered

Word level: to investigate compound words; to recognize and spell the suffixes *-tion -sion / -ible -able;* to understand how diminutives are formed

Lesson 1

Teaching Objectives

- *to identify social, moral or cultural issues in stories, eg the dilemmas faced by characters (T1)*
- *to investigate compound words (W11)*

Whole Class Shared Reading

Text level: *response to the story* **(20 mins)**

Read the excerpt to the class and ask the following questions:

- How has Danny cheated?
- What did Danny realize he would miss if he was blind?
- How does Mr King manage in his own house?
- What things does Danny hope will prevent him getting to the presentation?
- Why did Danny feel worse when he saw Mr King at the presentation?
- How does Danny hope to put things right?
- How does it all go horribly wrong?
- If you were Danny what would you do next?

Word level: *vocabulary extension* **(10 mins)**

Ask the children if they can find the following:

p54 a word to describe unclear vision (*blurry*)
an adjective to describe memories (*distant*)
p55 a phrase to describe Mr King's blindness (*the blankness in his eyes*)
a verb to mean looked quickly (*glanced*)
p56 a word that means between (*amongst*)
a word to describe a fat envelope (*bulky*)
p57 a word to describe silence (*stunned*)
a metaphor to describe how Danny's heart felt (*crash landing*)

Independent Group Task

Word level: *compound words* **(20 mins)**

Find six compound words in the excerpt (eg *eyesight, nothing, fingertips, Blackport, afternoon, football, anything, everybody, upset*) and then think of a linked compound word, eg *eyesight – foresight; nothing – something; fingertips – fingerprint* etc.

Lesson 2

Teaching Objectives

- *to identify the dilemmas faced by characters and to discuss how the characters deal with them (T1)*
- *vocabulary extension: words describing feelings and actions*

Whole Class Shared Reading

Text level: *identifying a character's dilemmas* **(20 mins)**

Reread the excerpt to the class and ask the children to think about the problems that Danny faces. Look at *Big Book* page 10. This sets out Danny's dilemmas and some of his solutions. Work through each dilemma ensuring the children understand the issues it raises. Discuss the solutions to each dilemma. Finally, decide what other dilemma Danny faces. Write this and his solution on the acetate sheet. Are there any more?

Word level: *vocabulary extension* **(10 mins)**

Ask the children to look through the excerpt for words and phrases which show how Danny is feeling. line 44 (*hunched*); line 53 (*pulled*); line 68 (*trudged*); line 73 (*turned miserably*); line 99 (*voice small and croaky*); line 105 (*voice clear and strong*); line 128 (*staring dumbly*).

Independent Group Task

Text level: *a character's dilemmas* **(20 mins)**

Consider how you would deal with Danny's dilemmas using PCM 1.

Lesson 3

Teaching Objectives

- *to recognize and spell the suffixes -sion and -tion (W9)*
- *to understand how the grammar of a sentence alters when the sentence type is altered (S3)*

Whole Class Shared Reading

Word level: *adding -sion or -tion* **(20 mins)**

Turn to *Big Book* page 11 which looks at the addition of *-sion or -tion* when changing verbs into nouns. Explain to the class the general rules about adding *-sion* and then fill in the gaps which ask the children to decide which ending to add.

Sentence level: *changing statements into questions* **(10 mins)**

Remind the class about how the grammar of a sentence can be changed when the sentence type is altered.

Change the following into questions and negative statements:

- *You have always been blind.*
- *My father was an artist.*
- *The money could buy Danny a computer game.*
- *You're a really good lad.*

Independent Group Task

Word level: *adding -sion or -tion* **(20 mins)**

Practise adding *-sion* or *-tion* to verbs to form nouns using PCM 2a or 2b as appropriate.

Lesson 4

Teaching Objectives

- *to explore the main issue of a story by writing a story about a dilemma and the issues it raises for the character (T11)*
- *to understand how diminutives are formed (W12)*
- *to understand how paragraphs are used to order ideas (T3)*

Whole Class Shared Writing

Text level: *considering a character's dilemma* **(20 mins)**

Remind the class about the dilemma that Danny found himself in at the end of the excerpt. Agree on the best course of action for Danny and jointly construct the next chapter of the book. Show the class how to use paragraphs to order and structure their material.

Word level: *forming diminutives* **(10 mins)**

Explain to the class that 'diminutive' means smallness. Write the following words on the board and ask the children what they think the words mean and which root word they come from: *booklet, rivulet, starlet, leaflet, duckling, fledgling, sapling, seedling, kitchenette, cigarette*. Ask the children what the words have in common.

Independent Group Task

Text level: *writing from another point of view* **(20 mins)**

Write a letter from Danny's Gran to her friend, describing what happened at the presentation.

Lesson 5

Teaching Objectives

- *to write critically about an issue or dilemma raised in a story, explaining the problem, alternative courses of action and evaluating the writer's solution (T8)*
- *to recognize and spell words with the suffixes -ible and -able (W9)*

Whole Class Shared Writing

Text level: *evaluating solutions* **(20 mins)**

Reread the opening of the story to line 8. Ask the children what they think Danny's options were at that point in the story.

Ask the children to look at the next solution that the author suggests. (Danny decides to give his winnings to a good cause.) Is it a final solution? Why does this lead to more problems? Ask the children how they think the author could end the story?

Word level: *-ible and -able* **(10 mins)**

Tell the class that adding *-ible* or *-able* to a noun changes the word into an adjective. There are far more words ending with *-able* than *-ible* but some very common words end in *-ible*. Turn to *Big Book* page 12 and show the class the list of common adjectives ending in *-ible* and their associated adverbs.

Ask the class to read them with you. What do they notice happens to the *e* when changing the word to an adverb?

Ask the children to fill in the adverb gaps. Then ask them to complete the sentences with the adjectives previously looked at.

Independent Group Task

Word level: *-ible and -able* **(20 mins)**

Correct the *-ible* and *-able* words using PCM 3.

Name ______________________

Literacy World

What Would You Do?

Danny is about to be given £50 as a prize for a painting he did not do.

How did he feel?

____

____

What did he do?

____

____

How would you feel if it happened to you?

____

____

What would you do?

____

____

____

PCM 1

Teaching objective: *Y4 T3 T1 to identify the dilemmas faced by characters and to discuss how the characters deal with them*

Links with **Unit 3 Lesson 2**

Name ________________________

Literacy World

Adding *-sion* or *-tion*

Remember: verbs that end in ***ss*** add ***-ion***
verbs that end in ***d*** drop the ***d*** and add ***-sion***
verbs that end in ***de*** or ***se*** drop the ***de*** or ***se*** and add ***-sion***.
verbs that end in ***t*** or ***e*** drop the ***e*** and add ***-tion***.

Change the following verbs into nouns by adding **-sion** ***or*** **-tion.**

suggest = ________________

complete = ________________

decide = ________________

revise = ________________

operate = ________________

express = ________________

explode = ________________

discuss = ________________

Using the words above, complete the sentences.

The class had a good ____________ about the value of zoos.

The man had a successful ____________ to remove his appendix.

The noise of the ____________ frightened the animals.

The teacher asked for ____________ for the class outing.

You must do lots of ____________ if you want to pass your exam.

The ____________ of the new road made the journey to school much quicker.

The ____________ to have a day's holiday was very popular.

The ____________ 'goodness, gracious me' made the children laugh.

Name ______________________________

Literacy World

Adding *-sion* or *-tion*

Remember: verbs that end in ***ss*** add ***-ion***
verbs that end in ***d*** drop the ***d*** and add ***-sion***
verbs that end in ***de*** or ***se*** drop the ***de*** or ***se*** and add ***-sion***.
verbs that end in ***t*** or ***e*** drop the ***e*** and add ***-tion***.

***Change the following verbs into nouns by adding* -sion *or* -tion.**

suggest = ____________________ erode = ____________________

decide = ____________________ revise = ____________________

excavate = ____________________ impress = ____________________

celebrate = ____________________ persuade = ____________________

Choose four of the words from the list above and write a sentence using the word.

1 ____

____

2 ____

____

3 ____

____

4 ____

____

Teaching objective: *Y4 T3 W9 to recognize and spell the suffixes -sion and -tion*
Links with **Unit 3 Lesson 3**

Name ______________________

-*ible* or -*able* Words

Underline the* -ible *or* -able *words Danny has misspelt and write them out correctly for him at the end of the letter.

Dear Tom,

I must tell you about a terrable thing that I did. You know how my Gran is always saying that I never do anything sensable and that I never really work hard. Well, she gave me this set of paints and expected me to try and paint a picture of her garden.

Well, I got bored and I went into next door's garden. There was such a lot of overgrown bushes that a hut was quite invisable and I nearly bumped into it. Inside, looking very comfortible was a really kind person called Mr King. He is blind but he used to paint pictures. I found one on the floor. It was unbelievibly good! I talked to him for a little bit and then I went back to Gran's.

When I returned I had Mr King's painting with me and Gran thought I was responsable for painting it. She entered it in a competition. It is just possable that I could win! I have a horrable feeling that I will get a prize and then I'll have to tell everyone what I did. I know Mum will be reasonible and understand that it was because I didn't want to let Gran down.

I'll let you know if the worst happens.
I'm in such a rush i hope this is readible.

Your best friend,

Danny

______ ______ ______ ______ ______

______ ______ ______ ______ ______

Unit 4

Hiker's Haikus and *Tomb Tunes*

Range: poems in different forms: haiku, epitaphs

Learning Outcomes

Text level: to recognize some simple forms of poetry; to understand poetic terms; to clap out and count syllables in poems; to write poetry, experimenting with different styles and structures; to describe how a poet does or does not use rhyme

Word level: spelling by analogy; practise compounding words by adding *-ful*

Lesson 1

Teaching Objectives

- *to recognise some simple forms of poetry (T7)*
- *to understand terms and identify them: rhyme, rhythm (T4)*
- *to clap out and count syllables in each line of poetry (T5)*
- *spelling by analogy (W3)*

Whole Class Shared Reading

Text level: *understanding the poem* **(20 mins)**

Read *Hiker's Haikus* to the class. Ask the following questions:

- What is a hiker?
- What way does the hiker think is the best way to travel?
- What does the hiker like to walk along?
- What do you think the hiker thinks of the motorway?
- What does the hiker like to do when he is walking along?
- What does he see and smell as he walks?
- What do you think he means when he says *'seasoned with bird song'.*
- Is the hiker happy or sad?
- Would you like to be a hiker?

Explain to the class that Haiku is a form of Japanese poetry. It looks very easy because it is usually very short, and very rarely rhymes. Each verse has three lines and they always follow a pattern.

Line 1 has five syllables
Line 2 has seven syllables
Line 3 has five syllables.

Haikus try to draw a picture in the mind with very few words. Read the poem again and ask the class to clap out the syllables.

Word level: *rhyming words and extending words* **(10 mins)**

Ask the class to give you the rhyming words from the poem in the first two verses (*feet, meat, streams, dreams*). Ask the children to suggest other rhyming words which follow the same letter pattern:
meat – beat, cheat, heat, bleat, pleat, neat, peat, wheat;
feet – beet, fleet, sleet, meet, greet, street, sheet, sweet;
stream – gleam, cream, scream, dream, steam, ream.
Write their suggestions on the board. Ask them which of the words can have suffixes added, eg *meeting, creamy, sweetly.*

Independent Group Task

Word level: *rhyming words* **(20 mins)**

Ask the children to look at the other rhyming words in the poem and create lists of words that sound the same and have similar letter patterns, or that sound the same but have different patterns.

Lesson 2

Teaching Objective

- *writing poems, experimenting with different styles and structures – haiku (T14)*

Whole Class Shared Reading and Writing

Text level: *evaluating haiku* **(10 mins)**

Ask the class if they can remember the form of haiku poems (5, 7, 5, syllables). Show them the haiku poems on *Big Book* page 13. Read the poems to the class and ask them to tell you which one they like best. Which one paints the best picture?

Text level: *writing haiku* **(20 mins)**

Explain to the class that they are going to write their own haiku about an animal of their choice. Working with a partner they should write the first line of five syllables. Remind them that the haiku does not have to rhyme.

Write their suggestions on the board and check that they have five syllables. Let the children continue to work on line two and line three. Discuss with the class their suggestions and poems. If possible make a class collection of the poems.

Independent Group Task

Text level: *Writing haiku* **(20 mins)**

Sort out and write haikus using the prompts on PCM 1.

Lesson 3

Teaching Objective

- *to practise extending and compounding words through adding parts eg -ful (W8)*

Whole Class Shared Writing

Word level: *adding -ful* **(30 mins)**

Look at *Big Book* page 14 . This demonstrates how nouns can be changed into adjectives through adding the suffix *-ful*. Work through the examples with the children and then ask them to complete the gaps. Test understanding of the words by putting them into sentences on *Big Book* page 15 and then test the spelling.

Independent Group Task

Word level: *adding -ful* **(20 mins)**

Make more adjectives by adding *-ful* and test understanding of their meanings using PCM 2a or 2b as appropriate.

Lesson 4

Teaching Objectives

- *to understand how a poet does or does not use rhyme (T6)*
- *to write poems, experimenting with different styles and structures (T14)*

Whole Class Shared Reading

Text level: *discussing epitaphs* **(30 mins)**

Read *Tomb Tunes* to the class. Explain that these are humorous epitaphs. People write epitaphs about people after they have died and most epitaphs are found on tomb stones. They are a form of poetry and they try to say something important about a person in very few words. Epitaphs sometimes rhyme and sometimes don't. Ask the class the following questions:

- Do these epitaphs rhyme?
- What is the rhyme pattern?
- Why does the poet say that Dad died?
- What was life like for the Mum?
- Why do you think the ten-year-old died?
- What do the children think *peevish* means?
- Why does the poet say that the last epitaphs must be a joke?

Ask the children to help you to compose some other epitaphs on the same lines.
You might start: *Here lies the body*
Of a pet called Jim...

Children should try to follow the rhyme pattern of the example in the anthology. Write the suggestions on the board. This could be the start of a class collection.

Independent Group Task

Word level: *experimenting with presentation* **(20 mins)**

Ask the children to choose the epitaph they think is the funniest and write it in their choice of presentation.

Lesson 5

Teaching Objective

- *to write poems, experimenting with different styles and structures (T14)*

Whole Class Shared Reading

Text level: *discussing epitaphs* **(30 mins)**

Turn to *Big Book* page 16 and read the *Nursery Epitaphs* to the class. Then ask the following questions:

- How do you know these are epitaphs?
- What did Little Boy Blue do in the original nursery rhyme?
- Why does the author suggest that Cinderella's sister might have killed her?
- What work did Little Bo Peep have to do in the original nursery rhyme?
- What did Miss Muffet do in the original nursery rhyme?

Ask the class what other famous nursery rhymes they know. Make a list of these rhymes on the board. Ask the children what they think could have happened to the nursery rhyme characters to cause their deaths.

Independent Group Task

Text level: *writing epitaphs* **(20 mins)**

Write your own *Nursery Rhyme Epitaphs* using the prompts on PCM 3.

Name___________________________

Writing Haikus

Remember Haikus have
5 syllables in line 1, 7 syllables in line 2,
5 syllables in line 3

Sort these Haikus into their three lines.

the fields are covered in white, Cold winds, soft snowfall, like a counterpane.

____

____

____

asking for the crumbs, The sparrow wants bread, jumps upon the seat and chirps,

____

____

____

Complete these Haikus.

The stream running past (5 syllables)

___________________________ *(7 syllables)*

___________________________ *(5 syllables)*

The teacher's waiting (5 syllables)

___________________________ *(7 syllables)*

___________________________ *(5 syllables)*

Teaching objective: *Y4 T3 T14 to write poems, experimenting with different styles and structures*
Links with **Unit 4 Lesson 2**

Name ______________________________

Adding -ful

Add the suffix -ful to the following words:

care ____________ hope ____________ success ____________

peace ____________ pain ____________ play ____________

power ____________ use ____________ beauty ____________

Use the adjectives from above to complete the sentences.

1 The __________ flower swayed in the breeze.

2 The children were very __________ not to drop any crumbs.

3 The garden was completely quiet and it was very __________ there.

4 The thorn had made Tom's finger very __________

5 The twenty gears on her bike made it very __________

6 The teacher was __________ that it would not rain on Sports Day.

7 The puppy was covered in mud and looked very __________

8 The football team were __________ in keeping the trophy.

9 The most __________ present his Dad had was a torch.

Teaching objective: *Y4 T3 W8 to practise extending and compounding words through adding parts eg -ful*

Links with **Unit 4 Lesson 3**

Name ______________________________

Adding -ful

Add the suffix -ful to the following words.

care ____________ hope ____________ success ____________

peace ____________ pain ____________ play ____________

power ____________ use ____________ beauty ____________

Choose five words from above and write a sentence using each of them.

1 ____

2 ____

3 ____

4 ____

5 ____

Teaching objective: *Y4 T3 W8 to practise extending words and compounding words through adding parts eg -ful*

Links with **Unit 4 Lesson 3**

Name ______________________________

Writing Epitaphs

Complete these epitaphs. They do not have to rhyme.

Here lies the body
Of a mouse by a clock

____

____

Here lies the body
Of the Man in the Moon

____

____

Here lie the bodies
Of Jack and Jill

____

____

Here lies the body
Of Old King Cole

____

____

Here lie the bodies
Of Three Blind Mice

____

____

Teaching objective: *Y4 T3 T14 to write poems, experimenting with different styles and structures*
Links with **Unit 4 Lesson 5**

Unit 5

My Pet and *The Who'z Who of the 'Horrible House'*

Range: poetry in different forms: thin poems, alphabet poems

Learning Outcomes

Text level: recognizing some simple forms of poetry and their uses; writing poems, experimenting with different styles; producing polished poetry through revision; describing how a poet does or does not use rhyme; understanding the term alliteration and identifying it in poems

Sentence level: identifying common punctuation marks

Word level: collecting and classifying words with common roots

Lesson 1

Teaching Objectives

- *to recognize some simple forms of poetry (T7)*
- *to write poems, experimenting with different styles and structures (T14)*
- *to identify common punctuation marks (S2)*

Whole Class Shared Reading and Writing

Text level: *discussing the poem* **(15 mins)**

Before letting the class open their anthologies on the relevant page tell them that the poem they are going to read is called *My Pet*. Encourage them to guess what pet it might be by giving them the following clues: *It doesn't fly, it doesn't sing, it isn't furry, it hasn't got a tail, it has no legs.*

When they have guessed what the pet is (a snake) ask them to predict how the poem might be presented on the page. Finally let them look at the poem. Read the poem to them. Why did they think the poet has chosen to set out the poem in this way? How else might he have set it out?

Ask the children to find the rhyming words and to supply the missing word.

What punctuation is used and what isn't used?

Text level: *writing a poem* **(15 mins)**

Create a thin poem about a stick insect or cat. Follow the frame of *My Pet*. Complete a first draft of the poem and then see if the class can build in the rhyme pattern of the original.

Independent Group Task

Text level: *writing a thin poem* **(20 mins)**

Ask the children to write their own thin poem about a pet of their choice.

Lesson 2

Teaching Objectives

- *to recognize some simple forms of poetry and their uses (T7)*
- *to write poems, experimenting with different forms (T14)*
- *to produce polished poems through revision (T15)*

Whole Class Shared Reading and Writing

Text level: *understanding the poem* **(15 mins)**

Look at the poem *Simple Seasons* on *Big Book* page 17. Ask the children to identify the form of the poem (*thin, acrostic*).

Read the poem to the class. Ask four children to each read a verse.

Ask the following questions:

- How do the swallows and primroses return?
- The poet has used only one word to describe the skylarks. Why has he chosen the word *up*?
- Why are the meadows described as *motley*?
- Why are the elms described as *regal*?
- Why are the apples described as *untold*?
- Why are the trees *unruly*?
- What has happened to the water?
- Why are the trees *naked*?
- What does the poet mean when he says the *earth rests*?
- Why do you think the poem is called *Simple Seasons*?

Text level: *writing an acrostic poem* **(15 mins)**

Create a class acrostic poem based on the letters of each season. Each line must be one word only. Write a first draft of the poem. Encourage the children to make revisions as more appropriate words are offered.

Independent Group Task

Text level: *continuing with acrostic poem* **(20 mins)**

Write an acrostic poem using PCM 1.

Lesson 3

Teaching Objective

- *to collect/classify words with common roots (W7)*

Whole Class Shared Writing

Word level: *words with common roots* **(30 mins)**

Look at *Big Book* page 20 which has lists of words which have common roots. Look at the words and explain to the children how looking for root words can help their spelling.

On the board write the headings *some, form, light, part*. Ask the children to offer as many words as they can that use the common roots and write them under the headings.

Independent Group Task

Word level: *words with common roots* **(20 mins)**

Make new words by adding to root words using PCM 2a or 2b as appropriate.

Lesson 4

Teaching Objectives

- *to recognize some simple forms of poetry – alphabet poem (T7)*
- *to describe how a poet does or does not use rhyme (T6)*
- *to write poems, experimenting with different styles (T14)*
- *to understand the following terms and identify them in poems – alliteration (T4)*

Whole Class Shared Reading and Writing

Text level: *discussing a poem* **(20 mins)**

Read *The Who'z Who of the 'Horrible House'* to the class. Check that the children know the meaning of the less familiar words (*eg umber = brownish, quagga = extinct horse*). Ask the children what they notice about the form of the poem (*it's an alphabet poem*). Ask the children the following questions:

- Does this poem look as if it rhymes?
- Does the poem rhyme?
- What is it called when lines are written using one letter of the alphabet for each word (*alliteration*).
- What do they notice about the letters of the alphabet? (*x is missing*).

Ask the children to identify the noun in each line. What two adjectives describe each noun? What do they notice about the second adjective? (*It is a colour.*) What action verb is each creature performing?

Text level: *writing an alphabet poem* **(10 mins)**

Ask the children to help you to write the first few lines of an alphabet poem that follows the alliterative pattern of *Who'z Who of the 'Horrible House'.* The second adjective need not be a colour.
For example: *an aggravating, annoying ant acting*
a big, boisterous bear balancing
Encourage the children to use the term 'alliteration'.

Independent Group Task

Text level: *writing an alphabet poem* **(20 mins)**

Tell the children to work with a partner and write either A–M or N–Z entries for an alphabet poem using PCM 3.

Lesson 5

Teaching Objectives

- *to recognize some simple forms of poetry (T7)*
- *to write own poems, experimenting with different styles (T14)*

Whole Class Shared Reading and Writing

Text level: *understanding a poem* **(15 mins)**

Look at *The Alphabet Speaks Up*! on *Big Book* pages 18–19. Ask the children what form of poem it is.

Read the poem to the class and check that they are able to understand how the names of the letters of the alphabet have been used to represent words or parts of words. Using the acetate sheet ask the children to tell you the full version of the letter/word and write this beside the letter.

Ask the children to read the poem with you again.

Text level: *writing a poem* **(15 mins)**

Ask the children to help you to write words using the letter name to represent part or all of a word. Work through the alphabet and write their suggestions on the board. Explain that the capital letter represents the name of the letter but that it is possible to use the lower case letters to represent the sound of the letter. For example *Km = came, Pp = peep*.

Independent Group Task

Text level: *writing a poem* **(20 mins)**

Write an alphabet poem using letter names.

Name ______________________________

Seasons Acrostic Poem

S ______________________________

P ______________________________

R ______________________________

I ______________________________

N ______________________________

G ______________________________

S ______________________________

U ______________________________

M ______________________________

M ______________________________

E ______________________________

R ______________________________

A ______________________________

U ______________________________

T ______________________________

U ______________________________

M ______________________________

N ______________________________

W ______________________________

I ______________________________

N ______________________________

T ______________________________

E ______________________________

R ______________________________

Teaching objective: *Y4 T3 T14 to write poems, experimenting with different styles and structures*

Links with **Unit 5 Lesson 2**

Name ______________________________

Literacy World

Root Words

Make new words using the root words below combined with those in the box. You can add to the beginning and the end of the words.

day	grown	how	dose	flow	head
where	body	hear	seas	one	times

some

____

____

____

____

over

____

____

____

____

cover	bathe	light	line	arm	coat
flower	pass	burn	ground	set	dial

under

____

____

____

____

sun

____

____

____

____

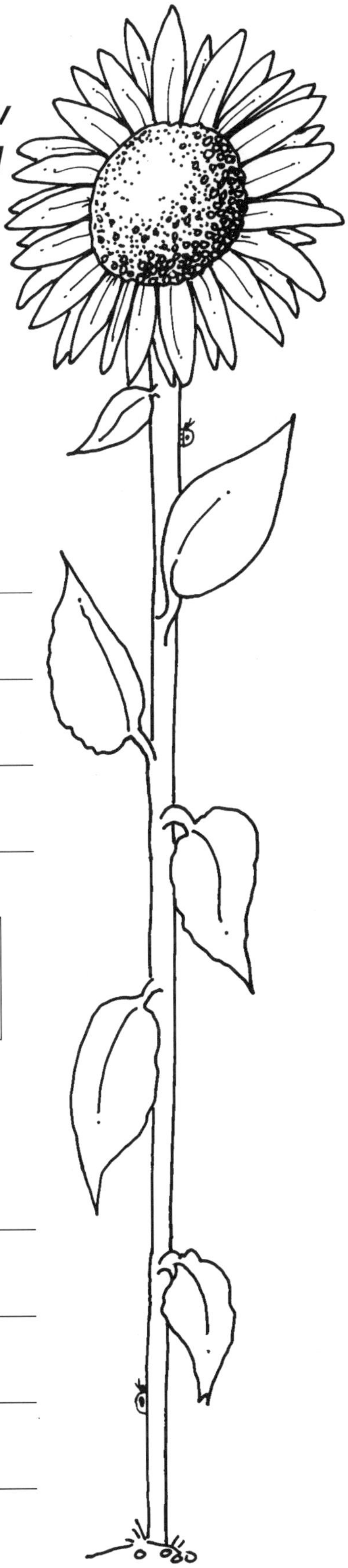

Teaching objective: *Y4 T3 W7 to collect/classify words with common roots*
Links with **Unit 5 Lesson 3**

Name ______________________

Root Words

Make as many new words as you can by adding to the beginning or the end of the root words below.

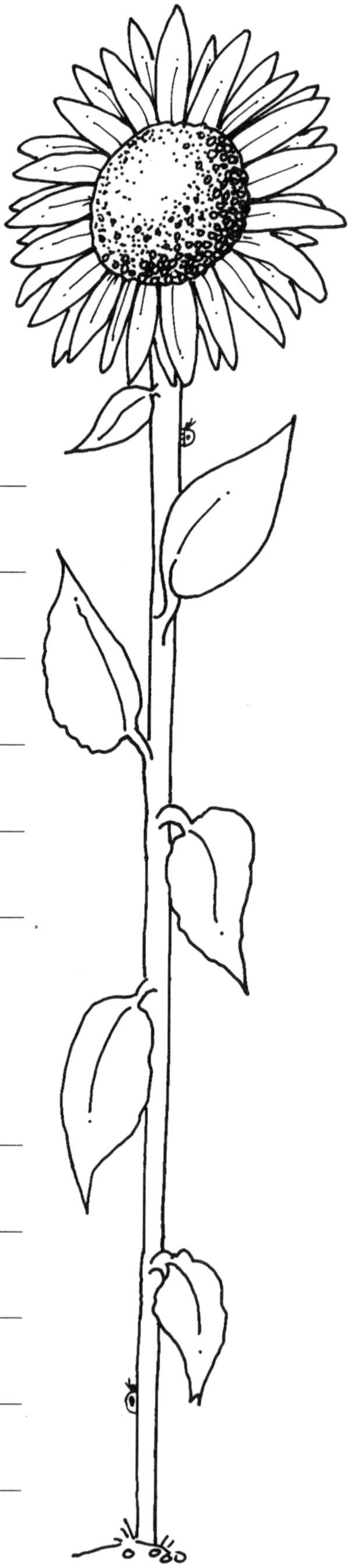

over

____

____

____

____

____

____

under

____

____

____

____

____

____

sun

____

____

____

____

____

____

foot

____

____

____

____

____

____

Teaching objective: *Y4 T3 W7 to collect/classify words with common roots*
Links with **Unit 5 Lesson 3**

Name ______________________

The Who'z Who of the 'Horrible House'

Write your alphabet poem about the Horrible House.
Work with a partner and write half each, A–M, and N–Z.
You might like to use the verbs in the box.

answering, bellowing, crying, decomposing, eating, floundering, gnawing, howling, imploring, jumping, kicking, laughing, moaning, nibbling, ogling, pecking, quarrelling, torturing, uttering, vivisecting, wailing, yowling, zooming

	Adjective	**Adjective**	**Noun**	**Verb**

Unit 6

As, As, As and *The Legend of the Lambton Worm*

Range: poetry in different forms: conversations, similes, ballads

Learning Outcomes

Text level: recognizing some simple forms of poetry and their uses; writing poems, experimenting with different styles; understanding poetic terms; revising poetry

Word level: practising extending and compounding words through adding parts; spelling by analogy

Lesson 1

Teaching Objectives

- *to recognize some simple forms of poetry (T7)*
- *to write poems, experimenting with different styles and structures (T14)*
- *to understand the following terms and identify them in poems – rhyming couplet (T4)*
- *to recognize and write similes*

Whole Class Shared Reading and Writing

Text level: *responding to the poem* **(20 mins)**

Before reading *As, As, As* to the class ask the children if they can remember what a simile is.

Read the poem to the class. Go over any less familiar vocabulary, eg *dour* (unfriendly), *scrunched* (crushed). Ask the following questions:

- What is the rhyme pattern of the poem? (*rhyming couplets*)
- Why has the poet linked *'slow and start'* and *'stopped and heart'* etc?
- Why do you think the poet repeats the words *'as boring as sir'* three times?
- What do you think it means when it says *'as there as a friend'*?

Divide the lines between the children in the class and ask them to read the poem again.

Text level: *writing similes* **(10 mins)**

Turn to the frame for creating similes on *Big Book* page 21. Ask the class to help you to write a first draft simile poem in the same form as *As, As, As.* Talk about rhyming couplets and encourage the children to provide rhymes for the second line. Revise the poem in the light of later suggestions by the class.

Then ask them to make suggestions for similes using the frame for *Our Country*. Ask the children which form they think is most effective.

Independent Group Task

Text level: *creating similes* **(20 mins)**

Write more similes using the prompts on PCM 1.

Lesson 2

Teaching Objectives

- *to recognize some simple forms of poetry (T7)*
- *to write poems, experimenting with different styles and structures (T14)*
- *to produce polished poetry through revision (T15)*

Whole Class Shared Reading and Writing

Text level: *understanding the poem* **(15 mins)**

Read *It's Raining Cats and Dogs* from *Big Book* page 22 to the class. Ask the children the following questions:

- What sort of poem would we call this?
- Do you find this an amusing poem?
- Why does Gran think the dog has got out?
- What did Mum mean when she said it was *raining cats and dogs?*
- What happened when Mum tried to explain to Gran that she meant it was raining hard?
- Why did Gran think she was talking about the vet?
- What happens when Mum tried to reassure Gran that the dog was fine?
- Why do you think the poet begins and ends his poem with *'It's raining cats and dogs'*?

Text level: *writing a conversation poem* **(15 mins)**

Ask the class to help you to write a conversation poem between two angry motorists both wanting the same parking space. They could interrupt each other before finishing their sentences.

Write the suggestions on the board. Encourage the children to suggest revisions to the first draft and discuss with them which is the better choice of words, or which words could be deleted to give the poem a tighter feel.

Independent Group Task

Text level: *writing a conversation poem* **(20 mins)**

Work with a partner to write a conversation poem between two friends at school or an adult and a young child.

Lesson 3

Teaching Objective

- *practising extending and compounding words by adding parts: -ly (W8)*

Whole Class Shared Writing

Word level: *making adverbs from adjectives* **(30 mins)**

Remind the class that adjectives describe nouns and that adverbs qualify verbs or adjectives. Many adjectives can be changed into adverbs by adding *-ly.*

Turn to *Big Book* page 23, which shows lists of adjectives which take *-ly* to become adverbs. Show the children the words and ask them to decide what normally happens to the spelling when a word ends in a consonant? What happens when a word ends in an *e?* What happens when a word ends in an *l?* Complete the gaps with the class.

Finally, say the following sentences to the class and ask them to say if the sentence has an adjective or an adverb in it.

The train arrived early. (adv)
The early train was in the station. (adj)
The journey was terribly slow. (adv)
It was a terrible day. (adj)
The girl had a soft ice-cream. (adj)
The boy crept softly towards the kitten. (adv)

Independent Group Task

Word level: *making adverbs from adjectives* **(20 mins)**

Change adjectives into adverbs using PCM 2a or 2b as appropriate.

Lesson 4

Teaching Objectives

- *to recognize some simple forms of poetry (T7)*
- *spelling by analogy (W3)*

Whole Class Shared Reading

Text level: *exploring ballads* **(20 mins)**

Explain to the class that a ballad is a simple poem that tells a story. In the past these ballads would be sung rather than spoken. These poems are often myths or legends that are very old.

Read *The Legend of the Lambton Worm* to the class and ask them to tell you the rhyme pattern of the poem and also to describe the story the poem tells.

Read the verse again to the children and ask them to clap the rhythm as you speak. Then read the verses again, but insert more words so that the rhythm is broken. They should tell you when they think the rhythm of the poem has been altered by you.

Word level: *rhyme* **(10 mins)**

Ask the children to tell you the rhyming words in each verse. When they have identified the word they should try to give you three more words that either rhyme or have the same letter pattern.

Independent Group Task

Text level: *prose version of poem* **(20 mins)**

Tell the story of the *Lambton Worm* in prose.

Lesson 5

Teaching Objectives

- *to recognize some simple forms of poetry (T7)*
- *to write own poems, experimenting with styles and structures (T14)*
- *to understand the following terms and identify them in poems – verse, stanza (T4)*

Whole Class Shared Reading and Writing

Text level: *discussing the poem* **(15 mins)**

Read aloud *When the Wind Blows* on *Big Book* page 24. Ask the class what the rhyme pattern is (*ABAB ACAC ADAD*).

Tell the children that when a poet uses a repeated line in a poem the 'verses' are then generally referred to as 'stanzas'. Ask the children the following questions:

- What effect does repeating the first line have on the poem?
- What things happen when the wind blows?
- Why is it a 'haven' inside but a 'battle' outside?
- Where would they like to be when the wind blows so hard?

Read the poem again and ask all the class to make the sound effects for the second line in each verse.

Text level: *writing a poem* **(15 mins)**

Ask the class to help you to compose a poem called *When the Sun Shines.*

Independent Group Task

Text level: *writing a poem* **(20 mins)**

Write a poem based on *When the Wind Blows* using the frame on PCM 3.

Name ______________________________

Similes

Complete these similes.

As large as ______________________________

A tall as ______________________________

As firm as ______________________________

As gentle as ______________________________

As beautiful as ______________________________

As strong as ______________________________

As nasty as ______________________________

Complete these similes.

The sun is like ______________________________

The ice-cream is like ______________________________

The old tree is like ______________________________

The train is like ______________________________

A toothache is like ______________________________

An eagle is like ______________________________

A frog is like ______________________________

Teaching objective: *creating similes*
Links with **Unit 6 Lesson 1**

Name ______________________________

Adjectives into Adverbs

Turn the adjectives into adverbs and write them on the lines provided.

The two friends walked **slow** ___slowly___ down the road.

Sudden ____________ they saw a bear rushing towards them.

The young man **quick** ____________ climbed up a nearby tree.

The older man lay **care** ____________ down in the road.

The bear went over to the man.

It sniffed **gentle** ____________ at the man's face.

The man did not move.

Then the bear went away.

The young man climbed **rapid** ____________
down from the tree.

'What did the bear say to you?'
he asked

'He told me not to walk with
a friend who is so **coward** ____________
that he leaves him to face
danger,' said the older man.

Turn these adjectives into adverbs:

brave ____________	safe ____________	kind ____________
honest ____________	quiet ____________	quick ____________

Name ____________________

Literacy World

Adjectives into Adverbs

Complete the chart by adding -ly to make adverbs.

Adjective	Adverb	Adjective	Adverb
quiet	*quietly*	safe	________
different	________	wonderful	________
brave	________	beautiful	________
honest	________	hopeless	________
usual	________	kind	________

Complete these sentences with an adverb of your choice:

The car went ____________ down the road.

The girl had painted her picture ____________.

The horse ran ____________ across the field.

The thunder crashed ____________ above our head.

The baby cried ____________ in his pram.

The fish swam ____________ down the river.

Teaching objective: *Y4 T3 W8 to practise extending and compounding words through adding parts: -ly*

Links with **Unit 6 Lesson 3**

Name ______________________________

Literacy World

Poetry Frame

***Write a poem based on the form of* When the Wind Blows.**

When the Rain Falls

When the rain falls

____

When the rain falls

____

When the rain falls

____

When the rain falls

____

When the rain falls

____

When the rain falls

____

Teaching objective: *Y4 T3 T14 to write poems, experimenting with different styles and structures*
Links with **Unit 6 Lesson 5**

Glossary

adjective: a word or phrase which describes a noun. There are different sorts of adjectives: number; quantity; quality; possessive; interrogative; demonstrative. They also have different degrees of intensity; nominative; comparative and superlative. Many adjectives can be turned into adverbs by adding *-ly*.

alliteration: phrases where the initial letters of words have the same phoneme: *round the rugged rock* etc.

analogy: a relationship between two things. In spelling this is often through common letter patterns.

antonym: a word with a meaning opposite to another: *light/dark*. Some words have more than one antonym.

calligram: a poem or word in which the presentation of the letters represents an aspect of the poem or word.

compound word: a word constructed from two other words: *schoolyard*.

concrete poem: a poem whose appearance or shape is part of its meaning, also called shape poems.

conjunction: a word which links phrases, sentences or clauses: *and, but, because* etc.

connective: words or phrases which link clauses, sentences, paragraphs and larger units of text. They can be adverbs *(suddenly)*, pronouns *(him)* and prepositional phrases *(on the other hand)*, as well as conjunctions.

couplet: two consecutive lines of poetry which are paired in length or rhyme.

diminutive: a term which implies smallness, often through addition of a suffix.

epitaph: words engraved on a tombstone, often giving information about the deceased.

fable: a short story which contains a moral.

free verse: poetry which is not organized using regular rhyme, metre, syllable count etc.

grapheme: written representation of a sound.

homonym: a word which looks and sounds the same as another, but has a different meaning: *pelt* meaning 'a hide' and 'to run fast'.

homophone: a word which sounds the same as another, but has a different spelling and meaning: *pair* and *pear*.

legend: a traditional story which may be based on historical events.

metaphor: a figure of speech which compares two different things, without using *like* or *as*: *her moon-shaped face.*

myth: an ancient story of gods and heroes, which often tries to explain how things originated.

narrative poem: a poem which tells a story, often in ballad form.

noun: a word which names people, places, things etc. Abstract nouns name concepts, ideas and emotions: *harmony, peace, love.*

onomatopoeia: words which sound like what they mean: *snap, crackle, pop.*

onset: the initial letter or cluster of letters in a word.

parable: a short story told to illustrate a moral.

paragraph: a section of a piece of writing which has a common focus. Also used when a new speaker begins on a new line.

phrase: a group of words without a finite verb forming part of a sentence, but which cannot be a sentence on its own: *The cat sat on the mat, because it was sleepy, the lazy animal.*

phoneme: the smallest unit of sound in a word. There are approximately 44 phonemes in English.

prefix: a letter string which is added to the beginning of a word to change its meaning: *un-believable, in-describable.*

preposition: a word used with nouns or pronouns to show time, place, position etc: *in, at, up, around.*

pronoun: a word which can replace a noun in a sentence: *she, him, its.*

root word: a word to which suffixes and prefixes can be added.

shape poem: a poem in which the layout of the words represents an aspect of the poem, also called concrete poem.

simile: a figure of speech which compares two different things using *as* or *like*. They often become idioms: *as daft as a brush.*

speech: direct speech gives the words actually spoken, indicated by the use of speech marks *(He said, 'Shut up!')*; reported speech does not present the actual words spoken and does not use speech marks *(He told me to shut up!)*.

stanza: a group of lines of poetry which forms a repeated pattern.

suffix: a letter string added to the end of words, which changes the status of a word (making a past tense or plural etc, such as *-ed* or *-s*), or which changes its word class (making a verb into a noun etc, such as *-er*).

synonym: a word which has a very similar meaning to another: *peace, harmony, accord* etc.

tense: indicates when something is happening, whether past, present, future or continuous.

verb: words which indicate doing, happening or being. Verbs can be in different tenses.

word play: where words are used to convey more than one meaning, spoonerisms, puns etc.